Money and the Modern Mind

Money and the Modern Mind

Georg Simmel's
Philosophy of Money

Gianfranco Poggi

UNIVERSITY OF CALIFORNIA PRESS
BERKELEY LOS ANGELES LONDON

University of California Press
Berkeley and Los Angeles, California

University of California Press, Ltd.
London, England

© 1993 by
The Regents of the University of California

Library of Congress Cataloging-in-Publication Data
Poggi, Gianfranco.
Money and the modern mind : Georg Simmel's Philosophy of money /
Gianfranco Poggi.
p.   cm.
Includes bibliographical references and index.
ISBN 0-520-07571-4
1. Simmel, Georg, 1858–1918. Philosophie des Geldes.   2. Money.
I. Title.
HG221.S56P477 1993
332.4—dc.20   92-32231
                                                        CIP

Printed in the United States of America
1 2 3 4 5 6 7 8 9

*To my fellow Fellows at the
Center for Advanced Study
in the Behavioral Sciences
1989–1990*

Contents

Preface

I completed the first draft of this book while holding a Fellowship at the Center for Advanced Study in the Behavioral Sciences at Stanford University. My stay at the Center was funded jointly by the National Science Foundation (Grant No. BNS87–00864) and by the Center for Advanced Studies of the University of Virginia, which awarded me a Fellowship for 1988–1990. I am greatly indebted to both institutions.

In the first half of 1990, the uniquely pleasant and supportive atmosphere of the CASBS, as well as the companionship of my wife, Pat, made it possible for this book to be drafted fairly rapidly. Unfortunately, after my return to Virginia the project lay fallow for a long time; and now that I look back on its genesis I realize uneasily how prolonged it has been.

I first read, and took a great number of notes from, *Philosophie des Geldes* in the mid-1970s. Unlike other books of mine, this one did not take shape after I had repeatedly discussed its content in the context of my teaching, since in the courses on "classical" sociological theory I gave several times at Edinburgh, and a few times at the University of Virginia, I never was able to devote more than one hour or so to *The Philosophy of Money*. In 1987, however, I was invited to offer the Mini-seminar in European Social Theory in the Department of Sociology at New York University (to which I am very grateful for that invitation). I gave as my topic "Simmel's *Philosophy of Money:* A Thematic Inventory," and while preparing the outlines of my seminar presentations I first experimented with the arrangement of the argument used in this book.

In fact, my treatment of Simmel's masterpiece, which is preceded by two chapters on the context of the work's genesis, does not really seek to take inventory of its thematic riches, but deals with its content in a relatively selective manner. Essentially, I seek to assist those who have not yet read *The Philosophy of Money*, and those who are in the process of reading it, in several ways. First, I focus their attention on four main themes. Two of these—the nature of action in general and economic action in particular, and the notion of objective spirit—are not explicitly "thematized" by Simmel himself. The other two *are;* they consist respectively in the nature of money (which is of course the book's eponymous theme) and in the nature of modern society. Second, I have sought to be more systematic in the treatment of these topics than Simmel himself is. (This, one might say, is not difficult, Simmel being notoriously unsystematic.) What this effort involves is largely a matter of assembling from the text numerous, fragmented, and dispersed arguments about a particular topic, and rendering them as components of a unified treatment of it. Third, my book is much shorter than *The Philosophy of Money*, and might thus assist potential readers daunted by the size of Simmel's work in learning what that book has to offer. I have also sought to express myself in a more accessible manner than Simmel does. He was a very accomplished and often particularly effective writer, as is apparent from the English translation of *Philosophie des Geldes;* but the philosophical tradition in which he wrote did not place a great premium on concise and plain phrasing. In any case, my friend Guenther Roth may be only slightly overstating the case when he suggests that today *The Philosophy of Money* is practically unreadable. By being both considerably shorter and (I hope) somewhat clearer than Simmel's text, my own may constitute for readers a less demanding way of familiarizing themselves with that text's contents. It will, however, best fulfill its purpose if it persuades some of them to themselves read Simmel on money.

Although, as I indicated, my first sustained encounter with *Philosophie des Geldes* had me grappling with Simmel's original text, on subsequent readings I used mainly the excellent English translation by Tom Bottomore and David Frisby published by Routledge in 1978. While drafting this book at Stanford, however, I availed myself of the just-published Suhrkamp edition, edited as volume 6 of the *Georg Simmel Gesamtausgabe* by David Frisby and Klaus Christian Köhnke (Frankfurt, 1989). In what follows, all quotations are in my own translation from this German edition, but page references are also given, in italics, to the English edition. This translation was reprinted in 1991, with much new and interesting editorial material by my friend David Frisby, to whom I am grateful for the help he has given me in writing this book.

Charlottesville, Virginia, March 1992

1

The Context

This is a book about a book, Georg Simmel's *Philosophie des Geldes* (*PdG*), first published in Berlin in 1900. I have undertaken to write about it at some length because, almost a century after it appeared, and several years after the publication of an excellent English translation (*The Philosophy of Money*), *Philosophie des Geldes* seems to me both significant enough and difficult enough to warrant an attempt to make it more accessible to readers. The attempt consists in selecting for attention some of the book's themes and in mapping out what I hope to be a manageable and rewarding reading itinerary through its lengthy, involved, and sometimes arduous argument.

Thus, I am discussing *The Philosophy of Money* in this book primarily because of its enduring significance as a text which provides a number of (as it seems to me) persistently valid or at any rate highly thought-provoking insights into a wide range of social phenomena. In doing this I am adopting what is sometimes called a "presentist" approach, not one which seeks primarily to locate and understand historically the text in question. That is, questions concerning the circumstances under which and the process through which Simmel produced *PdG*, the writings by others he may have used either as a source for his own argument or as a foil for it, the extent to which his ideas differed from what other authors of his own time were saying about money or about related phenomena—none of these questions, significant as they may be, are systematically entertained in what follows.

This chapter and the next, however, do address the fact that the book I discuss from a "presentist" viewpoint was written at a particular time and in a particular place and constitutes a significant moment in the personal and intellectual biography of its author. They do so by outlining first the broader social, political, and intellectual context of the genesis of *PdG*, and then the social and intellectual location of its author within that context.

I

Let us consider, then, the German Empire at the turn of the century—the high point of what is called the Wilhelmine era. The reference is, of course, to the emperor himself, Wilhelm II (1859–1941; *regnavit*, 1888–1918). Wilhelm, however, was also (indeed, in the first place) the king of Prussia. For the German Empire, at the time *PdG* appeared, had been in existence for barely three decades; whereas the Hohenzollern dynasty, of which Wilhelm was the head, had for as many centuries ruled Prussia and other eastern German lands as kings, and earlier yet as dukes. Besides, the whole German polity was strongly characterized, in its official constitution as well as through less visible but equally significant arrangements, by the dominant position Prussia held among the empire's component units (Bavaria, Württenberg, etc.).

Prussia, the easternmost component of the empire (though in 1815 the Rhineland had been added to its territories), had long been the largest and most powerful German state outside the Habsburg Empire. To build it up and maintain it in a region of Europe with contested boundaries, marked for centuries by ethnic, linguistic, and religious conflicts and by strong political rivalries, the Hohenzollerns had had to engage in the most exacting kind of power politics. Prussia had often had to deal, in complex diplomatic combinations and dangerous military confrontations, with bigger, better established, and wealthier European powers.

The Hohenzollerns' success, secured in spite of a number of setbacks, had been due largely to the distinctively authoritarian cast of the political structure they had created in the heartland of their territories (Brandenburg and Prussia) and then progressively extended to their further acquisitions. That structure concentrated all critical decisional faculties in the person of the ruling dynast, who exercised them without encountering the opposition or requiring the concurrence of other, independent powers, but nonetheless with the assistance of a relatively large body of politically committed nobles, the Junkers.

At that time most other German lands outside the Habsburg empire were fragmented into a large number of petty jurisdictions, often no bigger than a smallish town;[1] and even the rulers of larger territories, in conducting political business, had to take into account the privileges of diverse autonomous bodies.[2] Towns, villages, and corporations of various kinds rested their liberties, and their entitlements to intervene to a greater or lesser extent in the process of rule, on traditions evolved over the centuries in what had long been relatively wealthy and well-populated lands that possessed sizeable groups of literate burghers capable of forming and expressing opinions and of demanding their legitimate entitlements.

The Hohenzollerns' large and growing territories, however, were mostly located in what would now be called an "underdeveloped" region of Europe, lying east of the Elbe. The region had few large towns, which were mainly of recent origins, and most of it was sparsely settled by a dependent (and until the early nineteenth century enserfed) rural population, mostly grouped into large estates practicing relatively primitive forms of agriculture under the control and for the primary benefit of the highly privileged, landowning Junkers. Together, the ruling Hohenzollern dynasts and the Junkers ran those territories in the manner they thought was required by their prevailing social, economic, and cultural "underdevelopment" and by the threats and opportunities of power politics.

The Hohenzollern territories could remain politically unified, and grow, only if the state was militarily strong enough to withstand the opposition and the challenge of even larger, wealthier, and more established powers to the east, south, and west. Given the poverty of the region, the Prussian state could afford a strong army only if it constructed effective fiscal and administrative machinery for extracting resources from the population and deploying them for its own purposes. The Junkers, as a class, were central to this design. It fell upon them to lead the army and to construct and operate the fiscal and administrative systems necessary to build up and equip that army, as well as to secure orderly compliance from and maintain discipline among the population at large. This last task they performed in two capacities: as trained, hierarchically empowered and supervised *functionaries* running a sophisticated protobureaucratic system of offices that placed a premium on intellectual competence and on devotion to duty; and as *landlords* vested with wide judicial and police powers in managing the dependents of their estates.[3]

The army, under the direct command of the supreme ruler, was the pivot of Prussia's whole political existence and thus of its social life at large. It absorbed the great bulk of public resources, instilled in the subject population (until some time in the nineteenth century it would have been inappropriate to call it a "citizenry") a strong disposition toward unquestioning obedience, and trained into the members of its officer corps distinctive habits of selfless devotion to the public cause (embodied in the Hohenzollern sovereign) and of harsh, commandeering superiority toward everybody else. All other political arrangements—including, until 1918, an electoral system that vastly overrepresented the Junker element—were so designed as to assert the undisputed primacy of military considerations in the conduct of public affairs and to enforce the sovereign's personal will in matters of policy.

On that very account, Prussia was something of a constitutional archaism in nineteenth-century Europe, where most powers sought, in different ways and with different tempos, to modernize their polities. In other

Western countries, that is, an increasingly enfranchised citizenry, mostly belonging to a single nationality, was considered the key political constituency, and complex constitutional arrangements gave some leverage on policy to public opinion and to freely formed partisan alignments. In fact, Prussia appeared archaic even in comparison with other German, non-Habsburg lands, where the middle classes were having some success with similar forms of political modernization and were seeking to promote the formation "from below," through the pressure of opinion and political agitation, of a broader, unified German polity that would embody the new principles of national sovereignty, constitutionalism, liberalism, and even democracy.

However, it was archaic, autocratic, militaristic, antiliberal Prussia, ruled by a dynasty stubbornly undisposed to accommodate more than was absolutely necessary to the political spirit of the times, that—under the leadership of the greatest of all Junkers, Otto von Bismarck—performed the task of unifying Germany. And it did so through a sophisticated combination of the two counterbalancing devices of traditional power politics: diplomacy and war. But war played the more visible part in that combination: at Königgrätz in 1866 the Prussian army vanquished Austria, the other major contender for political leadership over the German lands, and in 1870 led the other German armies to a spectacular victory over the French Second Empire.

The fact that on January 18, 1870, the ceremony of the founding of the German Reich took place in vanquished France, and indeed at Versailles, in Louis XIV's own palace, signaled that the emergence of this powerful new empire at the center of Europe was the direct outcome of Sedan. The king of Prussia (then Wilhelm I) acquired the hereditary title of German emperor (Kaiser), some of whose powers (particularly those concerning army affairs and the appointment of the Reich's executive) paralleled those he possessed as king. Thus, and in other ways too complex to be reviewed here, the constitution of the new German polity established the dominance of Prussia—the largest and the strongest part of it, but by no means the most modernized economically, culturally, or politically.

The empire had a federal constitution, which reserved various powers to the autonomous institutions of its component territories; but at the federal level it provided no bill of rights and allowed no civilian supervision over military matters. Its chief representative body, the Reichstag, had legislative and budgetary powers (the latter very restricted as concerned military appropriations). But the federal executive was primarily responsible to the emperor, who freely appointed its prime minister—the chancellor—who was also the premier of Prussia. Complicated arrangements conferred on the Prussian legislature (outrageously *non*representative in its composition) indirect but highly significant powers over imperial affairs. Thus the German empire lacked the very substance of modern, representative politics: competition among parties over the electorate's support, resulting in the emergence of parliamentary majorities and/or coalitions and thus in the composition of an executive that forms policy and assumes responsibility for its outcome.

Political life in imperial Germany was thus, as it were, hollow at the center—if we take *center* as a metaphor for an arena where contrasting social interests,

availing themselves of public freedoms, organize themselves from the bottom up in order both to interact with
one another and to impinge upon the activities carried
out by state institutions at the top. Conforming to a
large extent, once more, with the Prussian model, the
empire constituted instead an *Obrigkeitsstaat*—an expression hard to translate, but whose semantic burden
lies probably in its first syllable, corresponding to the
English *over*. This term suggests a state in which authority is unmistakably and unapologetically concentrated at the top, and it expresses itself in an assured,
domineering fashion, for those "up there" (the authorities, the powers that be) are the sole guardians of interests—distinctively political interests—whose superiority over all others is (or had better be) undisputed. Thus
in the imperial *Obrigkeitsstaat*, collective forces such as
parties, which sought an investiture from below and expressly appealed to and represented interests of a social
and economic nature—perceived as nonpolitical because divisive—were made to feel ineffective, insecure
of their own legitimacy and relevance.

As a result, strong parties were first organized (overcoming much opposition and sometimes persecution
from the powers that be) among large social groups
which had reason to feel estranged from the existent order: the growing industrial proletariat, the Catholic pop-
ulace, and the middle classes. But, even as suffrage was
widened, these parties commanded only a (however sizeable and growing) minority within an electorate; the
majority supported, instead, relatively weak, poorly organized parties, which represented fairly different social
bases and policy options but were all basically at home
in the current dispensation, or were unwilling or unable
to challenge it in the name of liberal-democratic ideals.

For, after all, had not German unification, long a dream of some cultured, politically aware middle strata, particularly in the non-Prussian lands, eluded their own parties and movements, only to be achieved instead by authoritarian Prussia? Had not that achievement demonstrated the supreme significance, in the world as it is constituted, of power politics and the centrality to them of armed force, of which no better embodiment existed than the Prussian army, which now constituted the backbone of the Reich's armed forces? And since this newest great power had to maintain and assert itself in an inescapable contest with other great powers, did that not make domestic unity the critical political value, which would allow the Reich further to increase its military and industrial strength? Thus, was not the policy process the legitimate preserve of a strong executive, appointed by and responsible to the sovereign himself, and ably served by the Reich's uniquely competent and public-spirited officialdom, another precious legacy of Prussia's glorious past to the new German polity? Finally, had not the greatest Junker of all, Bismarck, guided the whole enterprise with the most consummate statesmanship, minimizing the leverage of parties and parliamentary institutions on policy, and showed the superiority of a strongly empowered, decisively led executive over an unsuitable liberal-democratic system, in which strong parties would endlessly enact their petty rivalries, neglecting the supreme concern of policy-making, the ceaseless pursuit of the nation's power in the context of world politics?

Indeed. Unfortunately, however, the first significant act of the new, young Hohenzollern dynast, Wilhelm II, had been to get rid of Bismarck (March 1890); and the two chancellors he had subsequently appointed before the end of the century (Caprivi and von Hohenlohe) had shown nothing like the same capacity for leadership, vis-à-vis the sovereign himself, who sought to exercise a personal rule for which he was both constitutionally unqualified and personally unfit, or the more and more self-important and intrusive military and administrative elites, or the increasingly restive and frustrated Reichstag itself. For Bismarck had qualities of genius, and a well-deserved personal standing, the sudden unavailability of which was causing the system to unravel.

By the time *Philosophie des Geldes* appeared, however, only particularly perceptive critics—among these a young contemporary of Simmel's, the economics professor Max Weber (1864–1920)—had perceived what a disastrous political vacuum Bismarck had left behind and the dangers of the course the ship of state was steering. Basically unreformed, and thus unmodernized, the empire was induced by the complacency and adventurism of the Kaiser, his court, and various military cliques, to foreign policy undertakings—such as the beginnings of a colonial policy and a naval arms race with Britain—which later would appear as self-damaging acts of hubris.

For the time being, however, most observers saw those undertakings as fully justified on various counts. First, they seemed to be just what a recently arisen world power owes itself as a means both of advertising its strength and of acquiring further power. Second, such initiatives were useful in deflecting domestic tensions and discontents and isolating the system's detractors, as they focused public attention on the empire's external successes. Finally, maintaining and increasing the army's already unequaled strength, and complementing it with that of a brand new, "state of the art" navy, served both to exhibit another significant feature of the empire—the strength of its fast-developing, technically innovative industrial economy—and to foster that strength by generating new, publicly underwritten investments and favoring the further, aggressive modernization of leading industrial sectors.

This last consideration needs further comment. By mobilizing and strengthening its considerable industrial resources, particularly in its western regions, the new empire had quickly become the home also of a fast-growing industrial economy, whose rates of growth and technological prowess had begun to threaten the so far undisputed industrial dominance of Britain. In Britain the original industrializing ventures had been centered on a product—textiles—whose requirements for capital, energy, technical know-how, and managerial skill were relatively small. Germany became the main protagonist of a second wave of industrialization—centered on steel and chemical products, and later on electrical products—whose requirements were much greater and could be satisfied only by much larger firms, much more heavily capitalized, with an intensified division of labor and more numerous technical and managerial personnel who would avail themselves of technical resources based on advanced scientific research. For this reason, in Germany's industrializing ventures the stock market and the banking system—which accumulated and deployed the requisite large amounts of capital—played a much more significant role than in the British case; and the same can be said of some major scientific and technical research centers, operating either within or, more often, alongside the university system.

Industrialization was a major aspect of the building
of the German Empire in which the Junker element
could not be directly involved, for it had its own economic home in the commercialized but otherwise relatively backward form of agriculture practiced on the
sandy soils of eastern Germany where the Junkers held
(on special, privileged terms) their noble estates. However, the socioeconomic and political equilibrium in
Wilhelmine Germany rested largely on a deal between
the Junkers and the business elite, sometimes referred
to as "the alliance between rye and iron."[4] The Junkers'
share of the deal was the maintenance of their semi-
feudal privileges as landowners and the protection of
the domestic price of their cash crops from the competition of better located and more efficient foreign producers, as well as the Junker element's undisputed priority as the stratum from which administrative and
military elites were recruited. The businessmen's share
consisted in the state's tolerance of their cartel arrangements and its positive assistance toward the building
up of heavy industry through favorable contracts connected particularly with the building of the railway system, electrification, and armaments.

Under this arrangement the Junker element also
played a significant, though somewhat indirect, role
in the promotion of industrialization. The operations
of the capital collecting and investing institutions
needed strong assistance from public administration
(which, as I have mentioned, the Junker element largely
controlled), and public policy was much invoked in
the prevention and repression of working-class protest
and in the management of other forms of dislocation
attendant upon the accelerated pace of German industrialization.[5]

Furthermore, the bourgeois element that was the protagonist of industrialization did not share the liberal political preferences of much of its earlier British counterpart. The bulk of it was, so to speak, more financial and managerial than entrepreneurial; it was highly dependent on the state both for the reasons I have just indicated and, more generally, because German industrialization took place in an explicitly protectionist framework that only the state could establish and police. The German bourgeoisie felt more threatened by working-class agitation and by the possibility of liberal-democratic institutions becoming established than did the business elites responsible for the the British industrializing push. While guiding a most rapid and impressive venture in economic modernization, it showed little interest in promoting political modernization. Essentially, the German bourgeoisie, and the diverse middle strata which took their lead from it, accepted (sometimes enthusiastically, less often with resignation or indifference) the mortgage laid upon imperial politics by the Hohenzollern dynasty and its Prussian inheritance.

This acceptance is all the more noteworthy if one considers that among the achievements of those social groups in the nineteenth century there was also a spectacular story of *intellectual* modernization. The story is too complex to be reviewed here, but two aspects of it may be mentioned. First, next to the traditional system of secondary and higher education, whose basic units were the *Gymnasium* and the university and which had long constituted the stronghold of German learning, there came to be established a new system, whose units were respectively the so-called *Realschule* (sometimes *Realgymnasium*) and the polytechnic or the *Technische*

Hochschule. The express institutional mission of the new system was the diffusion and advancement of the natural sciences. Second, a distinctive feature of German universities had long been that they emphatically promoted higher *learning,* not just higher *teaching:* that is, research was an integral part of their mission, next to the guardianship and transmission of the existent legacy of knowledge; and this principle held to some extent on both sides of the divide (for a long time a visible and invidious one) between universities on the one hand and the technical-scientific tertiary institutions on the other.

In due course, in the early twentieth century, a system of advanced research institutes gave further institutional expression to the commitment to advancing scientific and technical knowledge. This system—originally called the Kaiser-Wilhelm-Gesellschaft—was centrally established and funded, whereas the universities and the technical *Hochschulen,* like the primary and secondary schools, fell under the jurisdiction of the various *Länder* making up the empire. However, the universities in particular operated in fact as components of an unofficial empire-wide system: they routinely exchanged students and faculty among themselves, and competed for standing in an informal but well-recognized national hierarchy, which ranked sometimes whole universities, sometimes single disciplines across universities.

Together, its universities, technical institutions, and research centers made of Wilhelmine Germany an unequaled intellectual powerhouse; and in building and running those establishments not the Junker element but the bourgeoisie played the protagonist's role. The achievement in question was one of great complexity, and we would misunderstand it if we saw it exclusively as a matter of building up the scientific and technical infrastructure of a more advanced industrial system. In the universities, older, hallowed forms of learning—theology, law, philosophy, and the humanities—were still at the very center of the disciplinary map. But they were pursued in a new intellectual spirit, stressing rigorous, sophisticated scholarship to such effect that, for instance, by the end of the century classical scholars all over the world relied chiefly on the new editions of ancient Greek and Latin texts published by Teubner in Leipzig; and even in the scientific fields much emphasis was laid on basic, as against applied, research.

Furthermore, higher learning was only one aspect, however significant, of a broader intellectual and cultural development which by the end of the nineteenth century had made Germany into the most literate, cultivated, aesthetically sensitive and discriminating Western nation, and which again had various sections of the bourgeoisie as its protagonists. In the eighteenth century the German artistic genius had sought expression chiefly in musical form until Goethe had given it also literary expression; in the nineteenth, poetry and drama (and, to a lesser extent, fiction) had paralleled the continuing story of German musical creativity, sometimes merging with it (as in Heine's *Lieder* or, later, in Wagner's *Gesamtkunstwerk*). For some reason, the native figurative arts had never matched those attainments; but the great German galleries and museums had few rivals in Europe for the wealth of their collections. A large and sophisticated reading, and theater-, concert-, and museum-going public supported the institutions that produced and distributed all manner of cultural products and services. These included a publishing industry recognized to be the most active and enterprising in the world, whose products ranged from inexpensive editions of fiction and poetry in many languages to standard editions of texts from antiquity to a huge variety of newspapers and periodicals. And this "cultural industry" was not utterly separated from the institutions of higher learning: the great nineteenth-century German historians, for instance, from Ranke to Treitschke to Mommsen, had a large following among the broader reading public, and Mommsen's *History of Rome* was to gain him, besides the admiration of scholars of all nations, a Nobel Prize for literature. Earlier, the philologists Jacob and Wilhelm Grimm had produced, besides an enormous German dictionary, collections of folktales which in a matter of decades, in countless derivative versions, would feed the fantasy of children the world over.

Finally, the middle strata in Wilhelmine Germany saw themselves as the carriers not only of exacting standards of scholarly and scientific attainment and of aesthetic and intellectual cultivation but also of lofty moral ideals, centered on the inner values of integrity, hard work, sobriety, self-respect, honor, purity and strength of feeling, and duty toward one's family, friends, and colleagues. They were thus morally self-confident, whether or not they drew on Christianity as the source of their moral inspiration.

But somehow their capacity for sustained moral experience and moral discourse was exercised, in most cases, only in their personal lives, within the sphere of family and work, in the pursuit of cherished private values. Outside that sphere their capacity for self-reliance, their high evaluation of personal autonomy, and their sense of moral responsibility seemed to abandon them. At any rate, it did not inspire them to claim a right to involve themselves in the making of policy, to participate in the management of public affairs, to make demands on authorities, to monitor and criticize government actions, to take sides on current issues, to align themselves with like-minded people into competing bodies of opinion, or to assume political responsibility through organized parties. Their outstanding economic, intellectual, and cultural achievements and their keen moral sense somehow failed to empower them to take charge of their own political existence; they preferred to leave that to the established authorities.

After all, many of them felt, morality does not apply in that sphere whose concern is with the pursuit of national interest: and in the context of the sole significant and legitimate political game, power politics among sovereign nations, that pursuit finds in power itself its decisive medium and goal. But power is grounded in turn in the ultimate political resource, military force, which must be exercised, when necessary, exclusively according to the amoral criterion of its sheer effectiveness. Furthermore, the supreme political judgment is the judgment as to when force is to be employed against whom; and it can be best exercised by authorities which exercise as much leverage as possible over the whole political system and which need not concern themselves with the petty politics of sectional advantage and patronage in which parties indulge. To protect the private interests of individuals against depredations and abuses from authorities suffices "the law," which binds the authorities' activities to procedural criteria they know

how to apply rationally and which if necessary can be
enforced by courts. In any case, as long as most of the
elite political, military, and administrative personnel
was provided by the Junker element and was empowered by and responsible to the Crown, there was no serious danger either of those depredations and abuses
occurring or of serious misjudgments being made on
the weightier questions of power politics proper. Basically, the authorities in charge of the *Obrigkeitsstaat*
knew best what should be done and they were left to do
it, leaving individuals to cultivate and express their autonomy in the sphere of private interests and values.

II

Let me summarize and simplify further this already
highly simplified picture of Wilhelmine Germany. The
bourgeoisie played the protagonist's role in aggressively
modernizing the national economy; furthermore, it
guarded the unique intellectual and cultural heritage
of the nation and increased it by means of a set of institutions and practices that produced scientific knowledge and technical resources; finally, it self-consciously
guarded a moral legacy focused on values relevant to
the contingencies and demands of private existence.
The German bourgeoisie had not, however, acquired a
political significance in keeping with its own economic,
intellectual, cultural, and moral achievements but had
left the political system relatively unmodernized, to be
run according to its light by a Junker elite formed primarily by administrators, since the crown was held by a
sovereign with ill-grounded but assertive aspirations to
personal rule. (The Wilhelmine political system has

been characterized in our own time as "a bureaucratic monarchy ruling by its inherent traditional right.")[6]

Because it is so simplified, however, this is potentially a distorting picture.[7] At its center lies a national bourgeoisie which is, so to speak, inherently schizophrenic, because it does not care to match its success as an economic and intellectual modernizing class with equally self-confident and thoroughgoing efforts to modernize the political sphere. Such a view overlooks some features of the German bourgeoisie's attainments in scholarship and culture which, as it were, dissuaded it from seriously trying to claim its political birthright—a claim that the *Obrigkeitsstaat* would have resisted anyway. Some of those features have already been hinted at or implied above, but I shall discuss them at somewhat greater length because they shaped the intellectual field within which Simmel himself lived, and directly or indirectly affected much of what he thought, taught, wrote, and published.

Many leading representatives of German scholarship and science in Simmel's time expressly expounded the idea that they guarded a peculiarly valuable, distinctively German intellectual and cultural tradition, which enjoined them to distance themselves from (at any rate) the philosophical assumptions and the methodological strategies characterizing the work of their counterparts elsewhere, and especially in Britain and in France. More broadly, they seemed to feel that they would weaken and traduce the culture of Germany, the newest nation and great power in the West, if they relinquished their proud opposition to many aspects of Western culture at large.

That culture, they felt, had long since—at least since the Enlightenment—taken a turn that threatened intellectual insights and the aesthetic and moral values whose significance German culture uniquely cherished. Under the aegis of rationalism and positivism, Western culture enthroned as the sole medium of intellectual experience the cold reasoning power of the individual intellect, and directed it to seek abstract, universally valid generalities tested by mechanically collected data. In this way, it loosened the organic link between the individual's effort to apprehend reality and his/her location in a distinctive, historically determinate context, which both shaped and expressed (by, among other means, a language differing from all others in the ways in which it registered impressions and expressed thought) each nation's unique genius, its distinctive way of understanding reality.

Western culture failed to recognize the extent to which the givens of experience are organized for the inquiring individuals both by the particular worldview (*Weltanschauung*) they entertain (often unself-consciously, by virtue of spontaneous, unreflected affiliations) and by their powers of intuition and capacity for making sense of reality, for interpreting its inner meaning rather than objectively describing and accounting for its features. The express intent to produce through scholarly and scientific work precisely formulated, law-like, universally valid generalizations suggested that Western culture valued the intellectual enterprise chiefly to the extent that it afforded instrumental control over nature and society. Such control, furthermore, was ultimately intended to increase the individual's material well-being.

This preference neglected, or indeed repressed, the individuals' deeper human potential, and particularly their aesthetic sensitivity and moral sense, as well as their emotional oneness with and attachment toward those sharing their land, their language, worldview, cultural inheritance, history, and destiny. Indeed, as practiced in other Western countries, intellectual and cultural endeavors had become part and parcel of an increasingly massified, materialistic society, composed of atomized, competitive individuals no longer capable of spontaneous solidarities and able to coexist only under artificial conventions and arbitrarily produced rules. The European national cultures were thus severing their relations to their past, surrendering the inestimable legacies of wisdom and moral strength constituted by their homegrown folkways, mythologies, and histories, turning their back on their distinctive geniuses, and refusing to acknowledge and embrace their peculiar destinies.

One awkward aspect of Germany's begging to differ from mainstream Western ideas was that it entailed rejecting, or withdrawing from, parts of the German heritage itself, and particularly the autochthonous Enlightenment tradition culminating in Leibniz and Kant, with its overtones of rationalism and cosmopolitanism. But the German bourgeoisie negotiated this difficulty by appealing to a more recent part of that heritage: romanticism, a manifold of intellectual, aesthetic, and moral energies and dispositions that found its philosophical expression in German idealism (a movement also indebted to Kant on a number of counts):

> The central ideal in the . . . romantic world view is that of individuality. In the place of universally valid reason, whose general laws control and dignify the world's existence, there advances a world spirit which does not express itself in

uniform values, but in a plurality of individual historical configurations. The vision that characterizes German idealism is not that of a world of equal states which can maintain peace, but a world of different nations, rooted in tension and struggle. In this context the emphasis may lie on the muted fabric of the nation's spirit or on the creative energy of the great personality or on the transforming power of individual ideas—but again none of these interpretations appeals to general laws of reason.[8]

Inspired directly or indirectly by such views, many of the protagonists of the modernizing drive for which turn-of-the-century Germany was both admired (for its intellectual and aesthetic achievements) and envied and feared (for its industrial and military power) explicitly disassociated themselves from the values and assumptions which prevailed among their counterparts in other advanced nations. They refused to subscribe to the very project of modernity, to the confident expectations that intellectual and scientific advances and creative artistic experiences would bridge the remaining differences among various national traditions, that science would indefinitely foster progress, and universally emancipate individuals from the shackles of the past.

Although they held a position of growing prestige in the international community of their peers, German intellectuals and scholars specialized, as it were, in registering and bewailing the social and moral losses of modernization. They emphasized how unilateral and precarious the modernizing trends were and urged the "public mind" to rediscover the values of the premodern past, and especially the value of strong local and national attachments. By the turn of the century, of course, such "Catonian" motifs (to employ Moore's useful label)[9] were being heard among the intelligentsia of every Western nation.[10] In other countries, however (such as Britain, France, and Italy), they were sounded mostly by dissenting minorities; in Germany, they came from the elites. Not all groups spoke out to the same extent, of course: within the academy, in particular, the protagonists of the spectacular German advances in the "natural sciences" were much less likely to encourage their associates to follow a distinctively German path in their research and teaching. At the other extreme, in the humanities, in philosophy and law, those motifs were widely and aggressively played on by the recognized scholarly leaders.

In the middle, the social sciences registered a split between opposing tendencies; but even here most of the leading practitioners, particularly (not exclusively!) within the older generation, insisted that their German followers should eschew the path to scholarly and scientific advance favored by British and French students. There was, for instance, a significant, specifically German approach to the development of statistical science;[11] and the issue of how to study economic phenomena occasioned a particularly intense and protracted methodological argument. The initial issue in this so-called *Methodenstreit* was whether and how to develop a science of economics that rejected the marginalistic approach; but the dispute came to concern itself with a very broad spectrum of disciplines. To glimpse its significance, just consider the literal meaning of the label prevalently attached to those disciplines as a set—the *Geisteswissenschaften*, that is, "the sciences

of the spirit." An alternative, apparently less loaded label, *Kulturwissenschaften*, in fact had nearly as significant semantic resonances; for the German term *Kultur*
was laden with highly positive evaluative connotations,
best captured by the recurrent contrast between *Kultur*
(good) and *Zivilisation* (bad).

How convinced German scholars were of the distinctive nature and of the superior significance of their approach to those disciplines still shows in a 1923 book by
the philosopher and sociologist Hans Freyer (1887–
1969). Looking back on the great creative period of the
German "sciences of the spirit" in the late eighteenth
and the early nineteenth century, and focusing on one of
their legacies to later scholarship, the commitment not
just to the description and explanation of phenomena
but also to the understanding (*Verstehen*) of them,
Freyer wrote:

> The intellectual posture which the expression
> *Verstehen* designates is a key component of the
> ethos of the era during which our *Geisteswissen-
> schaften* became established—the era which
> goes from Herder, Winckelmann and Möser to
> Wolf, Humboldt, Niebuhr, Eichhorn, Savigny, He-
> gel, Schleiermacher, Bopp, and Jacob Grimm,
> and whose best products Dilthey selects and
> makes into a great theme of his own thinking. At
> that point, from the deepest powers of the Ger-
> man spirit there sprang what *Verstehen* stands
> for: a passionate commitment to the object of
> study, a capacity for universal empathy, a search-
> ing love for the distinctive mode of existence of
> historical phenomena, a controlled grasp of their
> inner forms. And this is an accomplishment of
> the highest ethical significance. For the historical

consciousness thereby attained is not a matter of
an alien spiritual fact passively reflecting itself
in an otherwise empty spirit, of history overrun-
ning life. What is involved, instead, is a highly
active relationship to the world of the spirit, comparable to the conquering raid which a creative
artist carries out in an uncharted region of the
soul. Doors are thrown open, peaks climbed,
depths plumbed. Enthusiastic commitment to
the matter under study . . . is here joined with
clear methodological awareness, creative exploration of the student's own subjectivity is joined
with the discipline of critical objectivity. And it
is no accident that the high season of our systematic philosophy, of our poetry and our music,
is attained at the same time as that of our
Geisteswissenschaften.[12]

The significance of the methodological debate concerning the *Geistes-* or *Kulturwissenschaften* is also suggested by the fact that history was among the disciplines
under discussion; for in the intellectual environment we
are considering history constituted, for all academics
other than the "hard" scientists, the master discipline,
whether "of the spirit" or "of culture," and one that
German scholars were held to be uniquely good at. Besides, the term *history* provided a label for *Historismus*—again, a distinctively German intellectual phenomenon, a complex set of widely shared philosophical
assumptions that not only sought to determine the approach to all phenomena studied by the disciplines in
question but also encompassed a conception of reality
at large, a vision of human destiny.

It may be useful, at this point, to consider briefly
what *Historismus* meant, if only because Simmel's

philosophical work has been authoritatively identified as a variant of it.[13] Unfortunately, it is not easy to spell out its meaning, among other reasons because it differs widely from that of the supposedly equivalent English term *historicism*. A few pointers will have to suffice. In the first place, *Historismus* enjoins the student of human affairs to attend first and foremost to what specific individuals or groups precisely located in time and space did, suffered, and uttered, to identify the specific course and outcome of their undertakings, and the distinctive nature of the arrangements they made, rather than emphasize what their experiences had in common with those of other individuals in different circumstances.

This methodological preference is justified because, in the second place, *Historismus* considers human beings as historical beings through and through. That is to say, what is significant about human beings flows not directly from abstract human nature but from the specific expression that the deeds and passions of individuals, bound in time and space, have given to the inherent potentialities of the species. Those deeds and passions, however, become embodied in artifacts of various kinds—from language to legal institutions to aesthetic principles—which both constrain and empower individuals other than those with whom they originated, shaping the circumstances under which people operate and the resources of which they avail themselves.

This view implies both that over time human beings' deeds and passions build upon the legacy of those who have preceded them, echoing and perfecting the specific expression they had given to human potentialities, *and* that at any given time concrete human collectivities embody different designs for living, and reflect different

patterns of knowledge and of morality. Thus, awareness
of the intrinsic "historicity" of human beings enjoins
those studying them to attend to both the continuity
and the diversity of historical experience. But the main
emphasis lies on the latter; it opposes any tendency to
overstress continuity and above all forbids considering
all of human history as the unfolding of a single design
or seeking laws purportedly regulating its advance
across the multiplicity and variety of time and space
bound experiences.

Thus the central intellectual mission of history itself
and of all other scholarly work inspired by *Historismus*
is to capture and convey the unique significance of
larger events—ranging from the creative impact of
"world-historical" individuals to the formation of populations with distinctive languages, myths, and institutions—rather than reduce them to instances of overrid-
ing generalizations. This commitment reflects itself—
and this is a third salient aspect of *Historismus*—in the
preference for a style of scholarly work aiming to interpret the significance of the object of study, rather than
just to describe its objective features or to account for
its course. The search for significance requires the student to identify as far as possible the subjective meanings individuals attach to their own doings and suffer-
ings, and most particularly the values embodied in the
beliefs and practices that individuals derive from their
group affiliations. To this end students must attune
themselves to the lived, meaningful experiences of the
individuals and groups they study and reproduce it
imaginatively within their own consciousness. At a
higher level, the historical significance of events can
only be identified by assessing their bearing on the

student's own values; for all values are produced within the matrix of a particular culture and acquire validity only by evoking the exclusive loyalty of individuals.

In sum, if I had to express in a single sentence the distinctive content of *Historismus* I would say that it teaches how significant the unforeseen consequences of contingent events can be. It sees human beings as exercising freedom in their choices, but reflects chiefly on the extent to which such choices on the one hand are circumscribed by the outcomes of previous ones while on the other they generate new constraints, irrevocably biasing the circumstances of future choices, and thus attain lasting consequences often out of all proportion to the entity of the original choices and in contrast with their intent.

This distinctive German view of the historical process was not an exalting one, in comparison with the sanguine "idea of progress"[14] which at the time underlay much writing in history and in other social and humanistic studies in other European countries and which attributed something akin to a providential design to the whole of human history, perceived as accelerating, in modern times, toward the universal triumph of European civilization. As we have seen, the dominant German emphasis lay instead on the shadow that falls between human undertakings and outcomes, and on the extent to which those outcomes condition future undertakings, attributing to different sections of humanity different strengths and weaknesses, assigning to each a different historical mission.

This vision could become an empowering one, instead of fostering resignation, only if those sharing it affirmed the peculiar significance of the German historical mission and committed themselves to its fulfillment. In the Germany of old, before unification, this would have meant simply that scholars should devote themselves to their calling in a particularly dedicated, productive manner, observing fastidious standards of intellectual craftsmanship, and proudly cultivating the distinctive strengths of German scholarship in their fields, as well as practicing the cherished bourgeois virtues of probity, honor, and aesthetic sensitivity. In the Wilhelmine Reich this private, workaday expression of commitment to the genius of German *Kultur* was often complemented by the scholar's enthusiastic assertion of the intrinsic superiority of German national values. Since, however, in a world of contentious sovereign states those values had to be upheld through political and military action, most members of the intellectual and academic estate shared in the uncritical endorsement of unchallengeable authority at home and of blustering might abroad which were characteristic of the country's political culture.

There are of course significant exceptions, and not only among natural scientists, such as the great medical researcher Virchow or the physiologist Dubois-Reymond, but also in other fields of scholarship. Theodor Mommsen, the great student of ancient history and Roman law, expressed his dissent from the political orientations of most of his colleagues and compatriots in his testament, written in 1899: "I have always been a political animal, and have wanted to be a citizen. But this is not possible in our nation in which the individual, even the best one, can never entirely transcend military subordination and political fetishism."[15] These exceptions apart, there seems to have been a significant connection between the very substance of German high academic thinking on one hand and the tendency of the German bourgeoisie to underwrite, rather than oppose, the archaisms of the imperial political structure on the other. In fact, it would have been surprising if it had been otherwise, considering that professors were themselves civil servants and that universities, when seeking to fill a vacant chair, had to obtain the consent of a minister in the *Land* in which they operated before appointing a candidate, after his scholarly qualifications had been thoroughly vetted by his professional peers.

The intellectual scene on which Simmel operated at the turn of the century, then, was marked by distinctive national traits, which make up something others have labeled "the German ideology." A recent, authoritative treatment of that ideology depicts it by means of a series of oppositions between an *echt deutsch* feature and one seen (and decried) as characteristic of modern, Western culture: romanticism versus the Enlightenment; a state based on corporate bodies (*Ständestaat*) versus industrial society; the middle ages versus the modern era; culture versus civilization; intimate values versus the external world; community versus society; and feeling (*Gemüt*) versus intellect.[16]

This last opposition indicates that the "ideology" in question must have introduced painful tensions into the mental world of intellectuals, scholars, and scientists; for, if they subscribed to the superiority of feeling over the intellect, they must have been condemned to practice their calling with a besetting sense of its ultimate insignificance in the higher scheme of things. In fact, if the intellect was inferior to feeling in its capacity to apprehend the core of reality and to impart moral meaning and esthetic resonance to individual existence, it was also inferior to naked power (ultimately, to the might of armies) in its capacity to realize the nation's interests.

To loosen those tensions, many German intellectuals and scholars invested the political realm with higher moral significance, charged it with the task of maintaining the autonomy and vitality of the German spirit itself and asserting its unique values. In this way, even scholars dealing with very mundane phenomena could convince themselves that they were dealing with higher matters, as long as they researched, taught, and wrote in a distinctively German fashion. Here, for instance, is Gustav Schmoller (1837–1917) extolling the particular virtues of the German variety of economics, *Volkswirtschaftslehre* (literally, "doctrine of the national economy"):

> Today's *Volkswirtschaftslehre* has matured; it has become an ethical conception of the state and society which opposes rationalism and materialism. Instead of becoming a mere theory of the market and of exchange, a kind of business economics, and thus potentially a weapon of the propertied class, it has again turned into a great moral and political science, which does not investigate only the production and distribution of goods or the value phenomenon, but also economic institutions, and which places man, rather than the world of commodities and capital, at the center of the discipline.[17]

It is difficult not to feel some annoyance at the complacency in this statement. Yet Schmoller was a scholar of towering stature who produced several works of great and lasting significance, especially in economic

and administrative history. Students of German intellectual history must in fact learn to live with the contrast between the admiration the writings they study
often inspire in them and the bemusement or indeed
sometimes revulsion awakened in them by the politics of the writers themselves, by the haughty sense of
superiority they often seem to derive from their affiliation with the German tradition, and, finally, by two
recurrent features of the style in which they express
themselves. One is the sense of smugness and self-
righteousness we detect in Schmoller's statement or in
the earlier quotation from a more recent author, Freyer.
The other is the writers' tendency to clothe their arguments in portentous language, to strike what impresses
most contemporary readers (at any rate if they are not
at home in German, or in the German tradition of academic writing) as a poor trade-off between profundity
and lucidity. Fortunately, as I hope this book will suggest, Simmel's *Philosophy of Money* shows only faint
traces of those two disconcerting stylistic features.

III

Having thus considered the broader context within
which *Philosophie des Geldes* appeared, I will very
briefly sketch a more proximate context: the city of Berlin, where the book was published and where its author
was born and spent most of his life. As in the 1990s Berlin is reestablished as the capital city of a unified Germany, it may also regain in the eyes of our contemporaries a status it had achieved during Simmel's lifetime
and lost in the wake of World War II—that of a great
European metropolis. Its development in the last de-

cades of the nineteenth century had taken place in a particularly self-conscious, aggressive manner; for Berlin built itself up as a metropolis in a country that had no tradition of metropolitan life. At the time of unification, Hamburg and Munich were only middle-sized cities by European standards; Berlin itself had only 826,000 inhabitants. But as the capital of Prussia it had already long been a significant political, administrative, and academic center. To these strengths, particularly after becoming the imperial capital, it added those of an industrial center: for instance, the great electrical firms of Siemens and AEG, the Schering chemical works, and the plants of the locomotive producer Borsig were located there. Under the empire, its urban development was accelerated (the population grew from 966,000 in 1874 to 1,677,000 in 1894)[18] and took early advantage of many innovations in transport, communications, sanitation, housing, and commerce. In 1896 Berlin offered a most suitable setting for a great international trade fair, which served to advertise its newfound vocation as (to translate directly the German expression) a "world city."

According to Gerhard Masur, whose book on the topic I follow here, "imperial Berlin" reflected and amplified the distinctive features of Wilhelmine Germany. In particular, during the so-called *Gründerjahre*, the few boom years immediately after unification, the capital saw particularly extensive and reckless real estate speculation and replaced Frankfurt as the country's financial center; there followed a sharp though not lasting decline of economic activity. At the same time, "Berlin society mirrored the hierarchical structure of German society in microcosm. . . . Berlin society was controlled in the main by an alliance between Junker aristocracy and bourgeoisie. 'The people' were given little voice and less power."[19] In particular, Prussia's peculiar electoral arrangements drastically underrepresented the lower orders, thus pushing their fastest growing component, the industrial working class, into the arms of the "antisystem" Social Democratic Party; and the town's mayor had to be confirmed in his office by the king (and emperor).

The military presence was very visible: the garrison was large, the elite regiments of the Prussian army being based in Berlin; the nerve center of the army, the General Staff, had its headquarters right in the middle of town, in the Potsdamerstrasse; and Wilhelm II had a veritable passion for military ceremonies and particularly for the great parades on the Unter den Linden avenue. A military style of interpersonal conduct, and particularly an arrogant, harsh way of expressing superiority and commanding subordination, was not only employed in the army itself, but also routinely adopted by military personnel in their dealings with the general public, and so it had contaminated social manners at large. As a result, modes of speech, posture, and demeanor originally exclusive to the barracks and the drilling ground had undergone a sometimes comical diffusion and exaggeration among civilians, occasionally evoking as a response, in the lower strata, a particularly sharp and bitter form of humor and repartee.

Yet, if much in the social structure and in the modes of conduct of imperial Berlin accounted for its sometimes being called "Sparta on the [River] Spree," on some counts the expression *"Athens on the Spree"* seemed equally appropriate. Some counts only, indeed:

for instance, although aggressively and imaginatively built up under the directorship of Wilhelm Bode, the Berlin museums and galleries had a long way to go before they could challenge those of Munich or Dresden; and book publishing in Berlin never matched, in quantity or in quality, the standards set by Leipzig. Yet the Berlin daily and periodical press was unparalleled anywhere in the variety and quality of its products, which included the best German review, the *Deutsche Rundschau*, and some of the world's most prestigious academic journals; the Berlin theaters saw playwrights and directors experiment with daring innovations in the content and staging of dramas; the town constituted for the greatest German novelist of the nineteenth century, Theodor Fontane, both a home and the theme of many of his books; and the Berlin Philharmonic Orchestra, founded in 1892, soon acquired a high international standing, which was nearly matched by the Royal Opera.

What is most relevant to our argument, however, is the fact that by the end of the nineteenth century the University of Berlin, founded only about a hundred years earlier and thus a relative newcomer among German and European universities, had become one of the world's greatest academic centers, on a par with Heidelberg, the Sorbonne, and Oxford. In some fields, in fact, it had no equal—fields as diverse as history and classical studies (with scholars such as Troeltsch or Wilamowitz), medicine (Koch), or physics (Planck and Einstein).

The scholarly and scientific achievements of the Berlin faculty were widely recognized and rewarded not only by colleagues and students but also by a broader cultivated public, the authorities of the empire, the

Prussian state, and the city of Berlin itself. To this day, many streets and squares in a large section of downtown Berlin, at the eastern end of the Kurfürstendamm, bear the names of nineteenth-century academic personalities, together with those of poets, novelists, and architects. What these symbolize has recently been sharply phrased by an Italian scholar: " 'German science' constitutes, in the official Wilhelmine ideology, one of the two fundamental instruments of the greatness of Germany and of her power in the world"—the other instrument being the country's industrial apparatus.[20] Not for nothing did the liberal-minded Dubois-Reymond refer to his colleagues on the Berlin faculty as "his Majesty's intellectual regiment of the guards."[21]

Masur writes:

> There was . . . one specific German quality to be noted in Berlin. The university was burdened with a political tradition to which most of its members adhered without reflection or compunction. The professors and, under their influence, the students shared a naive belief that their country had no parallel, and that it could count on a cloudless future. There was a deep seated complacency in the University of Berlin which played down the flaws of authoritarianism, militarism, and thinly veiled absolutism that characterized the second empire.[22]

In fact, a tone of bluster, of ostentatious self-assurance, dominated social life at large in fin-de-siècle Berlin, giving the town something of a parvenu quality, in comparison with the more settled physical and social atmosphere of the older European capitals, or for that matter of other German cities. Life in Berlin was exciting, but also restless and tense, among other reasons because society was sharply stratified, and its political structures, as we have seen, relatively unmodernized. In the next chapter we consider how our protagonist, Georg Simmel, stood with respect to the political and intellectual contexts we have sketched so far.

2

The Author and the Book

I

It is no coincidence that the first sustained treatment in German of the metropolis as a distinctive social and cultural phenomenon—"Die Grossstädte und das Geistesleben" (1903; "The Metropolis and Mental Life")—was written in Berlin by a scholar who had spent all his life in the city. Its author, Georg Simmel, had been born there in 1858. His parents' home was at the intersection of the Leipzigerstrasse and the Friedrichstrasse, in the very center of Berlin (the nearest station of the underground railway calls itself *Stadtmitte*, "middle of town"). The family was economically well off, the father being a partner in a well-established confectionery firm, Felix und Sarotti. (Sarotti chocolate is still being produced and exported.) He died when Georg was still young; but a friend of the family, the music publisher Julius Friedländer, adopted Georg, who was thus able not only to continue his studies but also (in due course, thanks to his inheritance from Friedländer) to maintain a comfortable upper-middle-class standard of living while pursuing, as we shall see, a somewhat problematic academic career.

At the time, many German students in the course of their degree studies attended courses in two or three universities in succession. It may be an indication of his particular attachment to his home town that the young Simmel did not; he enrolled at the University of Berlin in 1876 and remained there, attending courses in a variety of disciplines, including history, psychology, Italian literature, and history. On receiving his doctorate in 1881 he decided to make academic work his profession, in spite of some difficulties he had encountered with a dissertation on psychological and anthropological aspects of music.

Simmel's academic career was a difficult one. In 1885 the University of Berlin awarded him the title of *Privatdozent*, certifying that for the time being he had been found worthy not of an established position but of teaching courses whose remuneration would depend largely on the number of students they attracted. I say "for the time being," for the affiliation with a university entailed by a *Dozenz* served as a platform from which to launch a proper academic career. Normally in a few years a *Dozent* was appointed, in that same university or in another, an *ausserördentlicher Professor* (literally, "extraordinary professor") and subsequently an *Ordinarius*. Only the last, as the holder of an established chair, was a full-fledged, well-paid member of the academic profession, entitled among other things to supervise candidates for higher degrees.

It took Simmel fifteen years, much longer than the average, to advance from the junior position of a *Dozent* to the intermediate one in the academic hierarchy: he became an *ausserördentlicher Professor* in 1900, the year of publication of *Philosophie des Geldes*. He remained in this position for another fifteen years, during which he published, besides innumerable articles and essays, several books, most of which dealt with philosophical topics—although an important one was *Soziologie* (1908)—and established himself as a prominent feature in the capital's intellectual landscape. Only in 1914 did he become an *Ordinarius;* and the chair to which he was called was at a rather minor university, Strasbourg. Thus Simmel had to leave Berlin for a relatively remote place, where he remained until he died in 1918.

II

Simmel's private income protected him from the potentially awkward economic implications of an uncertain and slow academic career; furthermore, as we shall see, his long tenure in a junior academic position was offset to an extent both by his remarkable success in that position and by his renown in wider intellectual circles. On that account, one may well wonder why Simmel failed repeatedly (and sometimes shockingly) to qualify for chairs, at Berlin and elsewhere, in any of the fields in which he successfully lectured and published. There are four chief reasons.

In the first place, Simmel was of Jewish origins, and although his parents had been converted to Protestantism and had had him baptized in the Protestant church, he was widely identified, and not only by his detractors, as a Jew. Being a thoroughly secular person, he neither professed the faith of his ancestors nor observed their ritual practices; nevertheless in some circles it was held against him that he belonged—by virtue of his ancestry, but also, allegedly, by virtue of his appearance, his manners, his associations, his way of thinking, and the style of his intellectual work—to an ethnic minority which traditionally held low status and whose economic and professional accomplishments were resented by full-fledged members of Protestant Berlin society and of its university.

In Wilhelmine Germany there were no formal disqualifications attached to being of the Jewish faith, much less to being of Jewish origins. As early as 1812 Berlin Jews had achieved citizenship (such as it was in Prussia), and some residual limitations on the related rights had been set aside in 1848. Yet, "after centuries of official discrimination against Jews, the juridical act of emancipation could not effectively bring about their equality of entitlements in social terms. Through what has been called the 'suppression of the constitution by means of administrative practices,' Jews were still largely excluded from state offices, judicial positions, academic chairs and military careers, and remained second-class citizens through to the end of the Wilhelmine era."[1]

However, that exclusion was never total; and in any case, it was to an extent offset by the success Jews enjoyed in commercial and financial activities and as members of the free professions and of the performing arts. According to Masur, this was particularly the case in Berlin, which as a result saw a spectacular expansion of its Jewish population during the Wilhelmine era:

from 47,489 in 1871 to 151,256 in 1910. Jewish firms
were particularly prominent in finance, in the large-
scale retail trade, which they aggressively modernized
by establishing department stores, and in publishing.
And "the list of university professors, editors of maga-
zines, publishers of newspapers, who were members of
the Jewish citizenry of Berlin was a long one."[2]

On this account, Masur concludes that in the Wilhelmine era "Berlin . . . never became an antisemitic city";[3]
and René Koenig discusses the part played by Jews in
the history of German sociology: "Berlin, like all larger
cities, attracted relatively many Jewish families, for in
its metropolitan atmosphere, with its urbane tolerance,
they were more protected from the persistent and hurt-
ful discrimination practiced against the Jewish section
of the population in the smaller centers and in the
provinces."[4] For all this, there is plentiful evidence, in
Simmel's case as in others, that German universities
and other academic institutions, including those in Berlin, systematically placed obstacles on Jewish scholars'
roads to academic success—although those obstacles
were not always unsurmountable and those erecting
them almost never publicly revealed or denounced the
Jewish identity of those whose success they were seeking to impede.[5]

One can easily see motifs in the "German ideology,"
including some motifs sublimated and given dignified
intellectual expression in historicism, which would inspire in those subscribing to it a deep mistrust of, if not
active animosity toward, Jews. As we have seen, at the
heart of both that ideology and historicism lay an acute,
proud sense of the apartness of the German spirit with
respect to Western culture; and the Enlightenment was

often identified as the parting of the ways between the two. Basically, Western culture had committed itself to the project of "modernity"; German culture dissociated itself from that project, denouncing it as rationalistic, individualistic, secular, materialistic, shallow, and mechanical, and sought instead to remain in touch with deeper, spiritual, "organic" values. But the phenomenon of Jewish emancipation, particularly in Prussia, had been closely connected with the advances of the Enlightenment and the related reforms.[6] Secularized Jews in particular felt deeply grateful for the considerable advances toward civil equality made during the Enlightenment and generally espoused its values and assumptions.

Another distinctive feature of the German ideology and of historicism was the emphasis laid upon the distinctive history and unique destiny of each *Volk*, and of course on the superior significance of the German *Volk*'s history and destiny. Often that emphasis had distinctly nativist, indeed racist, undertones, which denied the validity or even the possibility of an affiliation between that *Volk* and people without German running in their veins. Jews were a prime example of such people, all the more to be mistrusted when they distanced themselves from their Jewish religious and cultural heritage and sought to identify themselves with Germany by their works—say, by writing as pure German poetry as Heine or as pure German music as Mendelssohn, or by celebrating German values and achievements in their scholarly writings.

Essentially, then, many established, powerful members of the university community considered Simmel a "stranger in the academy" and delayed his progress toward recognition, on account of his Jewish origins.[7] This consideration overlapped in their minds with a disapproval of Simmel's unconventionality. Encouraged perhaps by the fact that his livelihood never depended entirely on what he earned through his university work, Simmel, while otherwise following a mode of life suitable for a member of the cultured upper middle class in Wilhelmine Berlin, was something of a maverick in his academic activity. Many of his publications appeared in a variety of nonacademic periodicals. His academic writings themselves did not look like conventional academic essays or books: they had no apparatus of footnotes, did not refer to the sources of which the author had made use, and were written in a sophisticated, fluent, often brilliant style capable of capturing the attention of a wider public rather than in a style suited for addressing a restricted audience of scholars. The books themselves were often collages of relatively unrelated essays, with interspersed "Exkurse" which sometimes seemed simply to have germinated in the author's mind as he sought to arrange in sequence, under a single set of covers, a set of loosely related articles previously published in journals.

Above all, Simmel's courses and seminars and his writings ranged freely and unpredictably over a great variety of themes. Many of these did not fit easily within recognized scholarly provinces; they crossed or ignored disciplinary boundaries and did not lend themselves to the systematic treatment favored by established academics. What do you make of a junior colleague who this semester is offering a relatively conventional seminar on the philosophy of history or on logic, but last semester taught one on Rembrandt and next semester may, as the spirit strikes him, lecture on money, or on time, or on the psychology of women, or on relativism, or on Goethe? The further fact that this man had a penchant for criticizing and challenging his seniors, sometimes to their faces, did not endear him to many of them.

The resulting charge that Simmel was not a serious scholar and thinker in its turn often overlapped, in the minds of established academics who could and would hinder his career, with another consideration, which they were less likely to reveal to others or perhaps even to articulate to themselves: the man was a success. Newspapers and periodicals of all kinds, both German and foreign, solicited his contributions. He ran in his home a literary salon which attracted scholars of undoubted standing as well as members of the intelligentsia and fashionable artists and poets. Above all, he was a brilliant lecturer, who would frequently dazzle his listeners with the novelty of his insights but could also make them feel they were sharing in his voyage of intellectual discovery. Thus his seminars and courses successfully competed for students and auditors with those taught by other, senior professors; and this hurt some of them not only in their pride but also in their pocketbooks, for their earnings depended partly on enrollments.

In fact, Simmel had a veritable personal following among students at the University of Berlin—though, it was noted invidiously, this following was recruited disproportionately from a socially marginal, somewhat suspect audience, constituted of Jews, immigrants from Eastern Europe, and young women. This allowed his opponents to discount the significance of his success, and indeed to hold it against him, expressly or otherwise.

(Even the eminent church historian Ernst Troeltsch, on some counts fairly well disposed toward Simmel, was ungenerous enough to state that Simmel had, in his life-work, exercised his influence primarily upon "the higher levels of journalism": a judgment, Frisby notes, as damning as it was inaccurate.)[8]

A final factor hindered the career advancement to which, in the judgment of some figures of great academic standing, Simmel was entitled by his scholarly achievements. Early on, without renouncing his primary affiliation with the supremely well-established and respected discipline of philosophy, Simmel had committed himself to professing also an upstart discipline of suspect pedigree, and through the 1890s he had spent a considerable part of his undeniable talents as an author and lecturer fostering its public visibility and promoting its intellectual acceptability.

The discipline in question was sociology; and to become identified with it damaged Simmel, even in the eyes of senior colleagues who otherwise recognized and supported him. Sociology was a new-fangled field of study, not yet established in the university. Most self-respecting practitioners of the *Geisteswissenschaften* held it in very low regard for any number of reasons, including the distasteful association between "sociology" and "socialism"; the doubtful scholarly standing of Auguste Comte, who had given the discipline its hybrid name (etymologically half Latin, half Greek) and laughably vested it with the title of "queen of the sciences"; its recent popularity in Britain and in France through Spencer's writings, which subsumed all significant aspects of human history under an evolutionary account grounded on biology; its refusal to acknowledge the su-

preme significance of the state as the institution ordering and guiding society; the pacifist, cosmopolitan preferences of many of its practitioners; and its penchant for
vacuous generalizations which according to sociologists
amounted to universal laws governing social affairs.

This, then, was the discipline (using the term loosely)
which Georg Simmel, without ever ceasing to define
himself primarily as a philosopher, was seeking to legitimate by terming "sociological" the arguments he developed in many of his lectures and his writings.[9] In
fact his first book, published in 1890, dealt with "social
differentiation," and although here and in other writings Simmel adopted a psychological perspective along
with a sociological one, social differentiation was an expressly sociological topic of unmistakably Spencerian
lineage—and one whose significance was often reas-
serted in Simmel's later work.

In fact, Simmel's relationship to sociology was complex, and it changed over time. By and large it extended
over the two decades around the turn of the century,
and had its high point in the *Philosophy of Money* (1900).
By the time he published *Soziologie* (1908) his interests
were turning back from sociology toward philosophy—
with which Simmel had never ceased to be productively
concerned—although as late as 1917 Simmel unexpect-
edly revisited the discipline he had earlier abandoned
by means of one of his last writings, *Basic Questions of
Sociology: Individual and Society.*

In the 1890s, however, sociology was prominent
among Simmel's intellectual concerns. In 1895, he published an essay on "The Problem of Sociology"; in send-
ing a copy of it to Friedrich Althoff, a powerful and enterprising civil servant in charge of university affairs

within the Prussian administration, Simmel confidently stated: "Sociology is gaining more and more ground in the universities and it is certainly only a matter of time before this fact will be officially recognised everywhere. . . . I have contrived to substitute a new and sharply demarcated complex of specific tasks for the hitherto lack of clarity and confusion surrounding the concept of sociology."[10]

There are a few noteworthy things about this message. In the first place, insofar as the opening statement was true, Althoff, of all people, had no need to be told of, nor was he likely anyway to be delighted with, the expected advances of sociology. In the second place, the statement suggests Simmel's awareness that to make itself academically respectable sociology needed to, as it were, clean up its act concerning a matter as fundamental as the "concept" of it—and what indeed could be more fundamental for a German philosopher, particularly one affiliated with neo-Kantianism, as Simmel was, than a discipline's very *Begriff*? Finally, there is something brash about Simmel's declaration that *he* had already performed that much-needed job.

In fact, when we ask ourselves how Simmel had performed it, we realize that his own understanding of sociology was both sophisticated and complex on one hand, and astute on the other. Simmel was aware that some of the opposition to sociology derived from the sheer difficulty of finding a place for it in the relatively settled academic environment of the times, where each discipline occupied a fairly undisputed territory. Even if one discarded as impudent the Comtian claim that sociology was a kind of super-science, to which were subordinated all others, from physics to biology to economics, it was not clear how it could be coordinated with others, and particularly with such established disciplines as law, political science, economics, religious studies, and history.

Simmel addressed this difficulty—and sought to defuse the resulting opposition to sociology—chiefly by suggesting that the new discipline did not claim as its own object of study a self-standing set of social phenomena, identifiable by reference to their *content*, that is, to the nature of a distinctive set of interests in pursuing which individuals and groups interact with one another. Rather, sociology studies the *forms* of those interactions, the particular patterns individuals and groups generate in coming together and coming apart.

What makes such a focus worthwhile, according to Simmel, are three considerations. First, whatever interests they pursue, individuals and groups *must* pattern their own activities, and adjust them to each other's activities, in some form or other; at the very least, if they are to interact at all, they must interact in twos or threes or in greater numbers. Second, the basic forms of their interactions are the same across the diversity of interests individuals may pursue: the interests pursued by the Society of Jesus, for instance, differ from those pursued by an army, yet Ignatius of Loyola purposely organized the Jesuits on the model of a crack military unit. Third, the pattern in which individuals and groups interact has identifiable, material consequences of its own for the ways in which the originating interests can be pursued; thus, two hospitals may practice the same kind of medicine, but in different ways according to whether they are constituted as nonprofit organizations or as business corporations.

The upshot of these considerations, according to Simmel, was that sociology's mission is to identify empirically (for he conceived of it emphatically as an empirical discipline, unlike philosophy) the repertory of interaction forms open to individuals and groups in the pursuit of whatever interest they made their own, and to determine what constraints those forms placed on such pursuit. If so construed, sociology would not challenge the proprietary hold of older disciplines upon this or that aspect of the social process identified by its content; for its theme would cut across the established boundaries between them rather than displace them or supplant any of the disciplines.

The same relatively accommodating intent can be attributed to another way in which Simmel characterized the intellectual mission of sociology, supplementing his own prevalent emphasis on the forms of social life. He sometimes observed that the established disciplines dealt largely with the more massive and persistent social structures dominating the social landscape, from the churches to the state to business organizations to political parties to the army, and neglected instead less sustained and visible, more humble and down-to-earth episodes and configurations of interaction, such as friendships, sociable gatherings of various kinds, flirtations, exchanges of correspondence, quarrels, and acquaintanceships. Sociology could repair such neglect by exploring systematically these manifestations of social life existing, as it were, alongside and between the more imposing structures, and reveal how complex and sophisticated they were in spite of their apparent insignificance.

But this second understanding of sociology's mission was perhaps less accommodating with respect to other disciplines than might appear offhand; for sometimes Simmel moved from it to a third understanding, representing a greater threat to the other disciplines' sense of their own importance. He would suggest that the dominance of the intellectual map of society by the more imposing structures emphasized by those disciplines not only obscured lesser but not insignificant structures which existed, as it were, in the interstices between the former; and it also concealed the fact that the former structures *rested on* the latter, indeed *resulted from* the latter. For, after all, what keeps in operation something as imposing as a large business firm is, at bottom, a huge number of ongoing episodes of day-to-day, face-to-face interaction between individuals, a molecular process of mutual acquaintance, accommodation, cooperation, and conflict, which other disciplines have disdained to examine, and of which—once more—sociology may reveal the complexity and significance.

To sum up, Simmel worked up three different understandings of sociology which characterized it in relation to other disciplines, and which we can label respectively the *formal*, the *interstitial*, and the *molecular* understanding. In my view, I repeat, the last one was not quite as accommodating toward other disciplines as the other two; but Simmel's own emphasis lay on those two, and especially on the first. In any case, it is hard to tell what difference was made to his academic advancement by those understandings, jointly or separately, as opposed to by his espousal of sociology. After all, his commitment to sociology was always qualified, both because Simmel never—well, hardly ever[11]—defined himself as primarily and exclusively a sociologist and because he emphasized how distinctive his own conception of the discipline was. Besides, I repeat, that commitment was durable but not definitive: within a couple of years of publishing *Soziologie* and of taking an active part in the foundation of the German Sociological Association, Simmel undertook again to define himself exclusively as a philosopher. In any case, as we have seen, not just Simmel's commitment to sociology but also other aspects of his background and of his style of work made him a "stranger in the academy" and impeded his progress in his chosen career.

III

In fact, one may wonder whether Simmel was not something of a maverick in a broader sense, since to a considerable extent he dissociated himself from dominant intellectual tendencies in the academic environment of Wilhelmine Germany. Only some of those tendencies, mind you: for, as I have indicated, it is legitimate to think of him as a representative of *Historismus*—that is, of a set of positions widely prevalent among practitioners of the *Geisteswissenschaften* of his time. It was primarily his attitude toward modernity which distanced him from other representatives; as we will see in later chapters, his attitude was much more positive than that held by most of his colleagues.

Simmel shared and articulated many of the misgivings common in his generation toward some distinctive tendencies of modern life, such as the impoverishment of emotional sensitivity, the loosening of the sense of affiliation, and the diminished feeling of continuity with the past and of respect for traditional values. But he appreciated the intrinsic significance of the modern achievements with which those tendencies were associated. He valued chiefly the modern emphasis on freedom and encouragement of experimentation, which created many more opportunities for the expression and cultivation of individual preferences and potentialities.

An important aspect of this more favorable view of the modern experience was Simmel's appreciation for avant-garde developments in the arts and in poetry, which most members of the cultured upper-middle-class in Wilhelmine Germany saw as mystifying, unruly, barbaric, and a betrayal of all the aesthetic values they cherished. Artistic modernism seemed significant and valuable to Simmel for its relentless experimentation and for its ability to convey the distinctive tone and feel of modern existence, its restlessness, its fragmentariness, its ruthless denial of all that seemed solid and unproblematic to previous generations. The fact that he characterized himself, at any rate during one phase of his existence, as "a relativist philosopher" may have seemed well-nigh outrageous. It probably meant to many contemporaries that Simmel endorsed a modern tendency to authorize the holding of contrasting views on a given issue—a tendency that many considered a menace to the intellectual and moral nerve of individuals.

Simmel was not, however, necessarily *optimistic* in the face of contemporary developments. As chapter 7 shows, he was a highly aristocratic thinker, convinced that at best very few individuals, at the cost of much effort and suffering, could avail themselves of the opportunities for cultural development associated with modernity while resisting the materialistic seductions of modern life and the attendant tendencies toward moral stultification. In fact, in many ways Simmel shared the

distinctively autumnal feelings of his intellectual generation in Europe, its uneasy sense that the brave new
world the triumphant bourgeoisie had erected in the
course of the nineteenth century operated at a growing
cost to "the human soul," and in any case was less solid
than it appeared. The bitter critique of modernity developed by Nietzsche, in particular, undoubtedly exercised a great influence upon Simmel's views; and toward the end of his life, when practically all his lectures
and writings concerned philosophical as against sociological themes, he gave expression to these apprehen-
sions about the validity of the modern experience by developing his own variant of a "philosophy of life"
(*Lebensphilosophie*).[12] This variant emphasized life's inherent, irrational tendency to transcend all the forms,
material, social, and cultural, in which life itself unavoidably finds expression. For all this, throughout his
work, and most definitively during the early phase leading up to *Philosophie des Geldes*, Simmel was, so to
speak, more at ease with modernity, more at home
within it, less willing to criticize it and decry it, and by
implication better disposed toward Western culture at
large, than "the German ideology" allowed its spokes-
men to be.

   Before moving on to the brief account of the genesis
of *The Philosophy of Money* that follows, the reader may
wonder what its author was like—what manner of a
person was Georg Simmel? Perhaps because we still
lack a full-dress biography of him—a difficult task to
fulfill, not least because under the National Socialist regime most of the personal papers from his estates were
seized and subsequently dispersed or destroyed—it is
difficult to address that question. A relatively recent

German study of Simmel's philosophical work raises it but confesses to some bewilderment:

> If we put together the testimonials left by relatives, friends, colleagues, students, contemporaries, we find a number of sometimes contradictory indications concerning Georg Simmel. He is depicted by some as being tall and slender, by others as being short and as bearing a forlorn expression. His appearance is reported to be unattractive, typically Jewish, but also intensely intellectual and noble. He is reported to be hardworking, but also humorous and overarticulate as a lecturer. Finally we hear that he was intellectually brilliant, friendly, well-disposed—but also that *inside* he was irrational, opaque, and wild.[13]

Be that as it may, certain traits of Georg Simmel, the person, are well established by the available sources, and some have been mentioned or implied above. He had a relentlessly questioning intellect, with a self-consciously cultivated taste for surprising transitions in the analysis of the very different themes to which it applied itself; a penchant for paradox and for striking formulations; and a distaste, or perhaps an incapacity, for systematic discourse. He was able to uncover the complexities of apparently simple phenomena to an extent that somebody parodied by saying "Simmel will take no hair, and split it into four." He had a self-consciously refined aesthetic sense, which was evident in his speech and writing and in the range of his experiences as a concert-goer and museum visitor, at home and abroad, and as a reader. He enjoyed the advantages of a secure and comfortable economic position but never let them distract him from his vocation as a thinker and an author or lull him into a sense of complacency. His view of life, as we shall see in chapter 7, was in the last analysis tragic.

IV

But enough of the man; let us consider briefly the work with which the rest of this book is to be concerned. Three scholars—David Frisby in his preface and introduction to the English translation (1978) and more recently in his afterword to the second edition of it, and Alessandro Cavalli and Lucio Perucchi in their editorial introduction to the Italian translation (1984)—have most convincingly reconstructed the genesis of *PdG* and located it within the very large and diverse Simmel corpus. They have identified particularly significant themes (for instance, Simmel's relationship to Marx), recounted the reception of the book, and assessed its current status as an acknowledged, but on the whole insufficiently known and discussed, contribution to modern social theory. Much of what follows makes use of those scholars' invaluable writings, to which I refer readers seeking a more extensive discussion of those aspects of the book with which we are dealing.

In the last decade or so of the nineteenth century, Simmel, as a junior member of the faculty of Berlin University, became associated with an informal circle of younger scholars revolving around the great savant Gustav Schmoller. Schmoller then enjoyed as high a standing as any German scholar in the social sciences, and he shared the methodological, ideological, and political positions prevalent in his caste: it is on this account that I quoted him in the first chapter. In spite of his status he was a keen (though not uncritical) supporter of Simmel and encouraged his early scholarly efforts in the field of sociology.

In 1890, furthermore, Schmoller had Simmel address the participants in his political science seminar on "The Psychology of Money." This paper was subsequently published in an important journal Schmoller edited; ten years later, in his highly positive review of *PdG*, he suggested that the paper contained "the seed" of that book. Between 1890 and 1900 Simmel repeatedly raised the theme of money in a series of essays, the last few of which expressly presented themselves as forerunners of the more extensive treatment he intended to give that theme in a book. Frisby characterizes as "fragments" of the book eight of those essays, published between 1897 and 1900, which together account for nearly two hundred pages—over a third—of the book's first edition.

Over those same years Simmel shifted from "psychology" to "philosophy" in locating on the academic map his own concern with the phenomenon of money and the money experience, and he sometimes classified as "sociological" some of the problems he was raising—anything, one might say, to avoid locating his argument in the discipline more expressly and technically concerned with money, economics! In fact—as we know from a few letters he wrote to Heinrich Rickert, an important German philosopher of the time—Simmel, while writing *PdG*, had the most difficulty with those early sections in which he could not help confronting problems (such as that of *value*) more directly related to the *economic* theory of money. And, in the foreword to the book, he stated as explicitly as he could that "not a single line" in his inquiries was intended as a contribution to the treatment of money by economic science.[14]

As we shall see, Simmel felt much more confident about the bearing of his own line of argument on those associated with the Marxian tradition—as if he sensed that much in Marxism, too, did not exclusively or perhaps even prevalently discuss the specifically economic aspects of money and related phenomena, as much as it addressed their philosophical significance or their psychological and sociological implications. Marx and Adam Smith, Frisby notes, are the only economists to whom Simmel expressly refers (three times each); given his usual reticence about his sources, one can only wonder whether he consulted other, more recent authorities dealing with money.

The economists reciprocated Simmel's declared intent to stay off their turf by paying relatively little attention to *PdG*, on publication or later. Schmoller, as we have seen, reviewed it very positively; but he was chiefly an economic historian, not a practitioner of what one might today consider economics proper. One of the few reviews coming from *that* quarter was written by the Austrian Carl Menger, a leading proponent of marginalist economic theory and one of the protagonists of the *Methodenstreit*, in which context he had valiantly opposed Schmoller's insistence on the possibility and validity of a historical approach to economic theorizing.[15] Menger's chief objection to *PdG*, which he acknowledged to be a "comprehensive, quite brilliantly and stimulatingly written work," was that many of the problems Simmel had subjected to a philosophical analysis were in fact within the competence of economic theory proper, a field in which the author appeared "insufficiently well orientated."[16] In 1905, in fact, the distinguished German monetary theorist Georg Friedrich Knapp wrote in his foreword to his own main book on the topic, *Die staatliche Theorie des Geldes:* "The sociologist Georg Simmel's . . . profound work does not really deal with money as such, but rather with the sociological side of the money economy, so that I do not need to interpret my work as being in competition with it."[17] Yet in an incomplete piece of writing known in English as "Simmel as a Sociologist," Max Weber, who saw much to criticize in his contemporary but admired him greatly and did what he could, to no great avail, to foster his career, stated that "among economists . . . one can experience outright explosions of rage over him."[18]

On the whole, the book was widely noted and well received. Favorable responses came from various quarters, both in Germany and abroad. For instance, both Ferdinand Tönnies and his promising young colleague Alfred Vierkandt reviewed the book very positively. In 1902 *PdG* was to be the first major book read, with great admiration, by Weber as he began to recover from a painfully protracted and disabling depression. The editor of the *American Journal of Sociology* at the University of Chicago, Albion Small, arranged for the journal to carry two reviews of the book, the second of which was a translation of a review originally published in Germany. (The *AJS* had already published in English a chapter from the book, and was to remain for years, through a series of translations of his essays, Simmel's chief bridgehead in the English-reading academic world.) And among the philosophers who expressed their appreciation of the book was another University of Chicago professor, George Herbert Mead, who reviewed it quite positively in the *Journal of Political Economy.*

Finally, the reception offered *PdG* by other intellectual organs, not of the academic variety, also seems to have been quite warm; and Frisby reveals that somebody even thought of the book as "a source for the libretto for an opera by Hugo von Hoffmansthal," which, alas, was never written!

Of course, *habent sua fata libelli*—the fate of books is unpredictable. Emile Durkheim, whose *Année sociologique* had already published work by Simmel, gave a rather negative account of *PdG* in that journal, considering it, instead of a contribution to the sociology of economic life, "a treatise on social philosophy"[19]—not a term of praise coming from a man who was committed to differentiating his discipline from philosophy and who earlier had had reasons to consider Simmel as an ally in that enterprise. But these and a few other negative responses did not keep the book from being enough of a success—even in terms of sales—to warrant the publication of a new, slightly expanded edition by 1907. (The English translation is based on this edition, as is the German reprint I have used throughout.)

Let us now briefly survey the book's contents, before selecting for special attention a number of its themes in the rest of this work. *Philosophie des Geldes* is a large book—585 pages in the 1907 edition, 716 in the 1989 one. It is neatly organized into two parts, labeled respectively "analytic" and "synthetic": one, that is, dealing with the nature of money and the premises of the money phenomenon, and one dealing with its implications for other aspects of social life, and especially of modern existence. Each part is divided into three chapters of approximately equal length, and these in turn are subdivided each into three sections.

This neatly symmetrical layout of the work, suggesting on the face of it a systematic scholarly treatise, is in fact rather deceptive. As I have suggested above, Simmel was not a systematic thinker, and in *PdG* the transitions between one topic and another, or between one aspect and another of a given topic, are often as unpredictable in this book as they are in most of his other writings; and the scope of the argument, the variety of the topics into which it breaks up its subject, is wide enough to have made Durkheim consider the book, as we have seen, "a treatise in social philosophy." The reader can become aware of that scope by reading the numerous, abbreviated statements of the book's successive topics that make up its table of contents. The English edition has usefully reproduced these one-line statements also in the body of the work, inserting them at the appropriate points as subheadings of the text. This device, and even more so that of occasionally breaking up Simmel's overly lengthy paragraphs, render the English text much easier for the reader to navigate than the original, where often page follows page without so much as a paragraph break.

I refer to the table of contents of the English edition the reader keen to find out for himself what *The Philosophy of Money* was all about, and limit myself here to translating the chapter headings of the original:

ANALYTICAL PART

First Chapter: Value and Money

Second Chapter: The Value of Money as Substance

Third Chapter: The Position of Money in the Chains of Purposes

SYNTHETIC PART

Fourth Chapter: Individual Freedom

Fifth Chapter: Personal Values and Their Money Equivalents

Sixth Chapter: The Style of Existence

However, this list gives little indication of what Simmel really does in the book. After all, Frisby reminds us, it "emerged out of a whole series of essays published by Simmel over the preceding eleven years"; as a result, "the whole architecture of the work is not held together by a central argument but by myriad analogies and meandering enlightenments."[20] A reader who wants to sample one of the book's main themes—individual freedom, the subject of the fourth chapter—may take advantage of a publishing practice common at the time when *PdG* appeared. The author of a new book would sometimes buy space in a periodical and give notice of this work in a brief essay summarizing one or more of the book's arguments. What follows is my own translation (so far as I know, the first to appear in English) of Simmel's own promotion of *Philosophie des Geldes*. (Throughout, I have translated *Geist* as "spirit" and *geistlich* as "spiritual.")

PHILOSOPHY OF MONEY
by Professor Dr Georg Simmel (Berlin)

The title of this essay comes from a book in which I seek to exhibit the spiritual bases and the spiritual significance of economic life. I complement the position of historical materialism, which derives all forms and contents of culture from the economic relationships obtaining at a given time, by showing that in turn economic valuations and activities express more profound tendencies of the individual and collective spirit. Wherever one can ground aspects of intellectual, moral, religious, or aesthetic experience in the forces and transformations of the material sphere, it is also possible to excavate a further foundation of the latter, and to grasp the course of history as an interplay of material and ideal factors in which neither is always first and neither always last. I seek to establish this for the relationships between the forms of the economy with which we are familiar and the spheres of interest making up internal existence. In this way, I intend to foster the conviction that from any point on the most indifferent, least idealized surface of existence it is possible to plumb its farthest depths; that each of its particular aspects both contains and is contained by the totality of its meaning. Here, I will select, among the many demonstrations the book affords of these relations between what is most external and what is most internal, some of the connections that exist between the money economy and the development of individual freedom.

The personal subjection typical of the serf who owed his landlord certain determinate or "unmeasured" labors, or the delivery of a determinate portion of his crops, was relieved to the extent that those obligations were converted into monetary dues. For at this point the peasant was free, at least, in the choice of his activities, as long as they yielded the due amounts of money. On that account, the conversion into money payments was variously instrumental to the later emancipation of peasants from all services and deliveries. Also in the political sphere we encounter

something similar: the freedom of the English
people vis-à-vis its kings rests in part on the fact
that at one point it settled with them over certain
rights by means of capital payments. Exactly because there was something rather brutal and mechanical about this trading in the freedoms of
people, and not in spite of that, the trade signi-
fied a pure arrangement between the two parties,
in stark contrast with the king's sense that "no
piece of paper should stand between himself and
his people." On that same account, however, that
trade set radically aside all the imponderable
components of affect-laden relations, which—had
the liberties not been paid for in money—might
have led to their being subsequently withdrawn
or deprived of content. In the modern labor relationship it is indeed more difficult to recognize
the aspect of freedom resulting from the fact that
it involves money payments, for in fact the
laborer is as bound to his labor as the peasant to
the soil. Yet the frequency with which employers
change under a money economy, and the possibility of choosing them and changing them afforded
the laborer by the money form of the wage, confer
upon him, within his dependency, a wholly new
freedom, which we may acknowledge without denying that it often has little effect upon his material conditions. Indeed here, as in other spheres,
the connection between freedom and material
well-being is not as direct and necessary as one is
likely to suppose on the basis of aspirations, theories, and slogans. For as the employer acquits
himself merely by handing over cash, he too becomes free in relation to the laborer, whereas a
concern over his slaves and serfs would have obligated him to a greater extent.

Furthermore, insofar as it comes to depend on money, existence becomes more objective, and on that account again interpersonal relations, no matter how effective they are and how far they reach, confer on the individual a previously unknown freedom. The medieval corporation encompassed the whole person: a guild of clothmakers was not an association of individuals which pursued the mere interests of the clothmaking trade, but rather a living community which affected professional, sociable, religious, political and other concerns. In contrast with this unitary phenomenon, the money economy has made possible innumerable associations which either expect from their members purely money contributions or are aimed at purely monetary interests. This shows us one of the most significant cultural developments: the individual finds it possible to participate in an association whose objective goal he intends to foster or to profit from, but it is not the case that for the personality as a whole that connection involves a bond. Money has allowed the goal-oriented group to attain its pure form, the kind of organization which so to speak gathers what is impersonal about several individuals into a single activity; and it has taught the possibility of persons becoming unified while holding back all that is personal and particular about them.

The subjective feeling of freedom is sustained by the very fact that in a developed money economy man comes to depend on an ever-growing number of persons; for these have for the subject a purely objective significance, purely qua carriers of functions, owners of capital resources, means to the satisfaction of needs; whatever else they are as persons never comes into consideration.

Compared with modern civilized man, the member of an ancient or primitive culture depended on only the smallest number of individuals—but the narrow circle they made up involved them in much more personal terms. It was toward these personally familiar, and as it were irreplaceable individuals, that the old Germanic peasant or the Indian fellow clansman, or indeed still the medieval man, stood in a relationship of economic dependence; whereas, how many are just the "suppliers" on whom a man depends under the money economy! Yet he is incomparably more independent with respect to any single one of them, and he can change that one easily and at will. The significance of any single social element has been transformed into the unilateral, matter-of-fact significance of its performance, which for that very reason can be carried out also by other, personally different individuals, with whom we are connected by nothing else than an interest entirely expressed through money. But then freedom is not simply isolation, rather it is an utterly specific social relation: it is necessary that others should exist and be perceived if one is to feel positively free with respect to them. This happens most clearly when there do exist extensive relations to other people, purged however of all components of an utterly individual nature; influences, which however flow anonymously both ways; determinations, which however are indifferent to whom they affect. Given this sheer objectivity of the monetary relation, the personality of those involved appears wholly indifferent in spite of mutual dependency; and in this manner being-for-oneself, the individual's independence of anybody, openly attains the highest value.

Or one may consider the exceptional historical significance of the negative character of the freedom which money affords. In the eighteenth and nineteenth centuries various governments prohibited the "buying out" of peasants: this suggests a sense that a peasant would be unjustly damaged if one were to take away his land *even while compensating him fully in money* for it. For he would thereby gain a momentary freedom; but lose what confers value on freedom itself—the dependable object of his personal activity. For the peasant, the land still represented something other than its sheer patrimonial value; it meant for him the possibility of useful activity, a cluster of interests, an aspect of life toward which to orient himself—and all this he would lose the moment he possessed, instead of the plot of land, purely its value in money. He would gain thereby freedom from something, not freedom to something. We understand our own times better if we realize that the possession of money confers purely negative freedom with respect to everybody else, while making us depend on the condition that we hold it and use it. Ever since money has existed, everybody—by and large—has been inclined to selling rather than to buying. As the money economy develops, this inclination grows apace, and extends more and more to those objects which are not produced for sale, but appear as lasting possessions, and tend to fasten the personality to themselves rather than to free themselves of it through accelerated change—shops and factories, works of art and collections, landed property,

rights and perquisites of all kinds. Insofar as also
such objects remain for shorter and shorter peri-
ods in the same hands, and with greater and
greater speed and frequency the personality es-
capes from their specific configurations, this generates an extraordinary amount of freedom. Yet
these processes of liberation are unavoidably ac-
companied by the indeterminacy and the lack of
intrinsic direction characteristic of money, so that
frequently they become arrested at the moment
in which an uprooting takes place, and do not
lead to the development of new roots. Indeed,
since in the presence of very rapid monetary traf-
fics those possessions can no longer constitute a
fixed, stable content of existence, there is less and
less place for that intimate connection, fusion,
commitment, which assign constraining boundaries to the personality, yet at the same time give
it substance and sense. One can thus explain why
our own time—which on the whole, in spite of all
that still remains to be realized, possesses more
freedom than any other before—seems to find
such little joy in that freedom.

V

Having taken in this lengthy, "horse's mouth" statement of what awaits them in *PdG*, readers can decide
for themselves whether to have anything further to do
with the book. If this decision is positive, they may take
the plunge and start reading *PdG* itself. (Simmel, incidentally, advised perplexed would-be readers to start
with the last chapter, then read the rest, beginning with
the first chapter but possibly omitting the second. I

would again advise them to make early use of the excellent introductory material written by David Frisby for both editions of the English version.) Other readers, however, may read on here, following the selection and arrangement of topics of particular interest to myself (but, I hope, not only to myself) contained in the remainder of this book, which makes much use of quotations from the original (in my own translation) but sometimes brings to bear materials from other writings by Simmel himself or by other authors. Fortunately, these are not mutually exclusive alternatives; and readers may use what follows to compare the sense of what is significant about *PdG* gained from their own reading with mine, or alternatively move from my discussion to their own reading of the text.

One final word to those willing to read on. I shall not allow myself to be bothered, in what follows, by the question of whether what Simmel is writing, and what I am writing about *that*, constitutes "philosophy," "sociology," or "economics." In fact, when in 1895 Simmel decided to pick up the thread of his lecture of 1890 in the Schmoller seminar and to write a substantial book on money, he mentioned to Rickert "Psychology of Money" as his working title. And several readers (Tenbruck, for instance)[21] have authoritatively remarked that *PdG*, in spite of the title, and in spite of what Durkheim thought, constitutes Simmel's best contribution to sociology. If a reader really needs a label for what follows, I would reluctantly state that I am trying to select from *PdG* some themes of significance for *social theory;* but I shall not let myself be drawn into a further discussion of what that term means.

3

Action and Economic Action

In seeking to understand money as a central institutional phenomenon, Simmel places it against the background of a broader theme, the nature of economic activity. In turn, his treatment of the latter presupposes an even broader notion, that of human action in general. Although he does not discuss this notion as extensively and explicitly as he does economic activity, I shall make it my first task to assemble into a reasonably coherent argument various statements in *Philosophie des Geldes* that bear on the nature of action.

What does it mean to say that human beings are capable of *acting?* This is the central query of one of the most learned, original, and influential contributions to social theory of our century, Talcott Parsons's *The Structure of Social Action*, published in 1937.[1] Parsons sought to answer that query primarily by seeking to determine how it had been addressed (explicitly or implicitly) by some eminent social theorists of Simmel's own generation, two of whom (Weber and Durkheim) knew Simmel personally or expressly discussed his writings, including *PdG*. Parsons, however, for reasons which are of no concern to us here, considered the possibility of discussing Simmel also but decided otherwise. This was a redoubtable decision, in view of the fact that Simmel "does have a quite elaborate if not systematic theory of social action," the most significant components of which, I suggest, can be culled from *PdG*.[2]

Some of these components make up an elementary "philosophical anthropology"; that is, they seek to identify those persistent, universal features that distinguish the human species from others and characterize its relation to those other species, to nature, and indeed to the universe at large. Following Simmel's own usage, I shall often refer to the object of this inquiry as *man* (or *men*), since, whatever its supposed sexist overtone, *man* (like its German equivalent *Mensch*) has always had among its referents the species *Homo sapiens*, in both its genders.

In this perspective, action constitutes a distinctive relationship which members of the biological species *Homo sapiens* entertain with the rest of nature in the process of seeking, as the members of all species do, to maintain their own existence. What makes that relationship distinctive is, at bottom, the particular physical configuration which evolution has imparted to that species and which dictates to it, as to all species, how the universe appears to it and how to deal with the threats and opportunities that universe poses to individual members, to populations, or to the species as a whole. (99–100, 145; *106–7, 135*. Unfortunately, Simmel himself does not distinguish among these three levels of the relation between species and environment.)

Simmel does not state the particulars of man's evolved physical constitution which assign to him the burden or the privilege of dealing with nature also through action. Instead of describing human features in the matter-of-fact way of, say, comparative anatomy and physiology, Simmel's discussion of what makes action possible or mandatory for human beings emphasizes a rather baffling phenomenon: the ability of human beings to acquire subjectivity, that is, to perceive themselves as existing and operating in an environment perceived in turn as a set of objects. This ability is not a given of the human constitution as an opposable thumb is: rather, it is the outcome of a process of differentiation—a *social* process, as Simmel notes: "Only the knowledge of the other increases the knowledge of the ego [*Ich*]; indeed, the fundamental split of the ego into an observing and an observed part emerges only from analogy with the relationship between the ego and other personalities" (110; *112*).

Both at the level of the species and at the level of the individual, the point of departure of the process is a condition in which perceiving and being perceived, acting and being acted upon, the self and other entities, form an indistinct unity. At the point of arrival, that unity, or those unities, have been replaced by the interplay between two discrete, relatively self-standing entities. "The soul begins its existence in an undifferentiated condition, wherein the ego and its objects lie as yet unseparated, and impressions and images fill the consciousness without the carrier of these processes having

detached itself from them. . . . [But] a condition develops wherein man speaks of himself as 'I' and acknowledges objects which exist for themselves outside this
'I' "(30; *63*).

As to what leads humans to go from the first to the
second state, *PdG* is not very explicit, except for two
very broad points: first, that transition constitutes one
(the?) specifically human manifestation of a more en-
compassing process, the stubborn, multifarious self-
assertion of the phenomenon of life (655, *470*). Second,
the whole process takes place within, and by virtue of
the specific properties of, human mental activity. This
second point may seem like a truism, but Simmel imparts to it an idealistic twist when he attributes the process to the powers of the human "soul" (*Seele*. For instance, 584; *424* [but the translation is inadequate]). For
example, the objects which at the end of the process the
human subject confronts as entities irreducible to itself,
acquire their unity, as discrete assemblages of otherwise scattered sense impressions, only insofar as we
project into them the sense we have of ourselves as a
separate "ego" (*Ich*), and form them after our own image (629; *454*).

It is difficult to derive from *PdG* a more articulate view
of the process of differentiation which lies, as it were, up-
stream of the human capacity for action. Simmel designates several components, or aspects, or phases of that
process—soul, ego, spirit (mind), subject, consciousness—but never makes very clear how they relate to one
another. One may forgive him for this, however, if one
considers the intrinsic difficulty of the theme. Besides,
inadequate as it may be, Simmel's treatment on the one
hand independently confirms earlier insights into the

theme (for instance those concerning the mutual implication of subject and object that the young Marx had developed in his Hegelian phase, and that were not known
to Simmel himself),[3] while on the other hand it fore-
shadows the much more purposeful and elaborate treatment of these matters that the American philosopher
George Herbert Mead was to offer in the 1920s and 1930s.

The essential points common to Marx, Simmel, and
Mead are the following. Human subjectivity is the outcome of a process; it emerges only as a counterpart to
the developing awareness of objects; it involves the individual coming to perceive itself as an object by being
addressed as such by others. This feat rests on the mys-
terious ability of the human mind, or soul, or spirit, to
split itself up or to stand outside itself—not just to perceive, but to distinguish its perceiving activity from
that which is being perceived, and, above all and most
remarkably, to perceive itself as perceiving. To quote
Simmel himself:

> The fundamental capacity of our spirit [*Geist*]
> is that of judging itself, of imposing upon itself its
> own law. This does nothing but express or elabo-
> rate the primordial fact of self-consciousness. Our
> soul [*Seele*] possesses no substantial unity, but
> only that which results from the interaction be-
> tween the subject and the object into which it
> partitions itself. For the spirit [*Geist*], this is not a
> contingent form, which could be otherwise with-
> out modifying what belongs to our essence, but
> rather the spirit's own essential form. To possess
> spirit means nothing else than to be able to carry
> out this inner split, to make oneself into an ob-
> ject, to be able to know oneself. . . . The subject

endowed with soul knows itself as object and the object as subject. (118–19; *117–18*)

Simmel's insights into these matters do not acknowledge the role played by social activity to the extent, and in the depth, that Mead's do. However, as we shall see in chapter 4, Simmel emphasizes much more than Mead does the extent to which some at least of the objects on which the subject tests its subjectivity are themselves the *product* of its activity or of that of similar subjects.

Simmel construes action in a way that is basically individualistic. Human individuals, like all forms of life, must maintain their existence by dealing actively with their environment; action is the form of activity specific to man, for it presupposes (though it also feeds back into) the process of subjective development we have just briefly considered. Action can only take place in a universe traversed and structured by subject/object relations, and these so far as we know are exclusive to human beings.

Of course human beings interact with the environment in other ways as well, through forms of activity which they share with other animals—and particularly, one presumes, with higher animals. Simmel does not indicate how types of activity, and the "mixes" among different types, vary on the evolutionary scale he apparently posited among animal forms and at the top of which he placed humans. Rather, as was usual in his generation of scholars, he operates with a crude dichotomy between instinctual and noninstinctual activity: humans share only the first with other animals. However, Simmel elaborates this distinction by laying over it another between activity primarily "pushed" by preexistent conditions and activity primarily "pulled" by envisaged, not-yet-existent consequent states, or goals (*Zwecke.* 254; *204*).

Thus, Simmel characterizes action in the first place as goal-oriented activity, engaged in on behalf of end-states which we opt for rather than under the pressure of blind impulses (*Triebe*) or by adapting to established constraints. One might say, adopting an insight of a French contemporary of Simmel's, George Sorel, that by the same token action is essentially *free* activity: "We must abandon the idea that the soul can be compared to something moving, which, obeying a more or less mechanical law, is impelled in the direction of certain given motive forces. To say that we are acting, implies that we are creating an imaginary world placed ahead of the present world and composed of movements which depend entirely on us. In this way our freedom becomes perfectly intelligible."[4]

Simmel, however, is not so sanguine. He qualifies his characterization of action as activity oriented to envisaged end-states rather than flowing from existent conditions, by remarking that all activity necessarily involves the expenditure of energy and manifests causal forces producing effects in space and time. In the case of action this unavoidable causal aspect of activity is put in motion by subjective processes. But while these may involve yet nonexistent states of things, they must themselves be carried out before the expenditure of energy in which, I repeat, all activity consists. "Our acting is never caused by a goal in the sense of something which is yet to be, but by a goal in the sense of a physical-psychical energy which *pre*exists the acting" (295; *230*). On this account, "since the outcome must be

present in the form of psychical activity, before embodying itself within the objective realm, a strict causal
connection is by no means dispensed with" (254–55;
205). (Cavalli and Perucchi suggest that with this argument Simmel may have opened the way for a thesis developed by Max Weber a few years later, to the effect
that two distinct ways of accounting for sociohistorical
phenomena, that aiming as explaining [*Erklären*] and
that aiming at comprehending [*Verstehen*] a given phenomenon, are not necessarily mutually exclusive.)[5]

As Simmel construes it, furthermore, action necessarily involves "effort" (to use Parsons's terminology),[6]
that is, a purposive expenditure of energy to modify or
eliminate existent states which do not conform with the
envisaged goals (258–59, 382; *207, 423*). Even more important, action has an unavoidable temporal dimension
(258; *206*) which is the locus of the *means/goal relationship*. For although so far we have construed action
chiefly by reference to the end-states to which it is oriented, its most important structural feature is that such
states can only be attained via means, that is, by inter-
posing between the existent and the opted-for state of
things one or more activities that neither result "mechanically" from the former state nor find their justifi-
cation in themselves as the latter state does.

In fact, an end-state is a goal only insofar as it requires to be attained by employing means, through effort, and in the course of a temporal process: "One may
speak only in a very qualified sense of God as having a
final goal with respect to the world," since "for a God's
power no temporal or objective interval may exist between the formulation of a will and its realization,"
whereas human action inserts itself between these two

moments, and is nothing but "the overcoming of obstacles that cannot exist for a God." "For God there is no goal, because for him there are no means" (258; *206–7*). In the context of a further discussion of the means/goal relationship, the comparison between man and God is complemented by considering also other animals: "The notion of means characterizes man's position in the world. Unlike the animal he is not tied to the mechanism of instinctual life and to immediate wanting and enjoyment, but neither does he possess the immediate power we attribute to a God, such that His will is identical with its realization" (264; *211*).

Any sustained examination of the means/goal relationship must emphasize the element of *plurality*, and thus of choice, selection, that the relationship entails. In the first place, it belongs to the very concept of a goal that it is a state attainable through more than one means; a goal that is, so to speak, totally soldered with one and only one means becomes indistinguishable from it. In the second place, it belongs to the very concept of means—as is clear, in particular, in the case of "tools" as a paradigmatic category of means (261; *209*)—that it can assist in the attainment of more than one goal. In the third place, what constitutes a goal with respect to a certain number of means can in turn serve as a means to a number of further goals.

Simmel particularly insists on this third point, which he expresses by speaking repeatedly of "chains of goals" (*Zweckreihen*), the increasing length of which he considers as an essential aspect of the process of civilization (492; *360*)—an insight much elaborated some decades later by the German sociologist Norbert Elias.[7] With increasing length comes increasing complexity, for each means that serves as link in a chain oriented to one goal may also serve in the attainment of other goals; besides, a given goal may be the end-point of a number of chains.

Rather than considering at length the treatment *PdG* accords the means/goal relationship (see the whole opening section of chapter 3 of *PdG*) I would like to emphasize for a moment the broader concept of *mediation*, which Simmel uses occasionally but without sustained attention to its meaning. The German expression for it—*Vermittlung*—and that for "means"—*Mittel*—overlap much more obviously than do their English equivalents. Besides, *Vermittlung* and related expressions carry a larger and denser semantic load, in the language of German philosophy, than *mediation* does. In German writings within the dialectical tradition, in particular, one often finds expressions such as "man *mediates* his own existence." What does this mean?

Without using that expression in *PdG*—much less expressly reflecting on it—Simmel throws light upon it at various points, for instance when he remarks that man does not perform labor (and labor is a distinctively significant form of action) the way the flower performs its blossoming (58; *423*). There are three significant, overlapping differences here. First, we do not think of the flower as engaging in effort when blossoming; whereas our notion of labor (and indeed, as I suggested, that of action) definitely entails an element of effort. (Jesus specifically contrasted the lilies of the field, on this count, with men's anxious and painful busy-ness.) Second, we generally think of labor as carried out instrumentally, that is, not for its own sake but with a view to a further goal; and again, this does not apply to the flower's blossoming. Although it generally does have important biological consequences, these (so far as we know!) are not envisaged or subjectively entertained by the plant. Third, we conceive of the activity involved in the flower's blossoming as wholly programmed by nature, whereas most aspects of laboring are consciously arranged, resulting from choices made if not by the laborer himself then on his behalf by other subjects.

One might construe this last point solely as reasserting the human privilege of freedom extolled in my previous quotation from Sorel. On more sober consideration, however, labor appears as a type of action which distinctively reflects necessity, since we mostly engage in labor under the pressure of need (576; *418*). Yet, if needs must, what constitutes need and how a given need is to be met are for humans highly variable matters. In other terms, necessity encloses and determines human beings less tightly than it does other beings.

Mediation means that humans can intervene, interpose themselves more contingently and inventively, and thus more diversely, in making their own existence possible than other species can; their own purposeful activity can make more of a difference to that process. But they can do so only because, to return to Simmel's argument about the emergence of subjectivity, they can to an extent disengage themselves from the unceasing buzz and flow of sensation and the dumb pressure of need to which they are exposed, instead of responding to them immediately and thus nonmediately. Simmel makes this point by referring to two previous characterizations of man—as the "goal-setting" and the "tool-making" animal—and then offering his own: man as the "indirect being" (264–65; *210–11*).

Later, however, he suggests that man might also be characterized as "the objective animal" (385, *291*). For, as we have seen, human beings can perceive themselves within the continuum of reality as discrete entities counterposed to other entities (including some which they perceive as similar to themselves),[8] and can act upon, and by means of, such entities as well as be acted upon by them. It is this ability to establish a *distance* between themselves and the rest of reality that allows humans to differentiate reality into conditions within which they must act, goals toward which they opt to act, and means via which they choose to act. In fact, they must distance themselves also from the raw sensations and the utterly spontaneous emotions that aspects of reality awaken in them if they are on the one hand to acquire selfhood, on the other to apprehend the significance of those aspects (41; *71*). "What distinguishes man from the lower animals in purely psychological terms, is the capacity for objective consideration, for disregarding the ego with its states and impulses to the benefit of sheer objectivity" (384; *291*).

We can think of action as an "arc" (*Kurve*) spanning the distance which subjective development establishes between subject and objects, and traveling that distance two ways: the arc first goes from the subject to some aspects of the objective world, modifies them or absorbs them, and then returns to the subject. Because of the return leg, as it were, of the arc's itinerary, the relationship between selfhood and action is a reciprocal one: action both presupposes and generates selfhood, understood as a person's awareness of itself as a discrete, self-activating entity (254–56; *206–7*).

Let us now consider more closely the subjective processes involved in action. *PdG*'s treatment of this theme is neither extensive nor systematic; but a few useful points can be derived from it. Obviously, among the human capacities on which action is grounded, the ability mentally to project a future is critical, because the future is the locus of possibility. But *possibility,* Simmel reminds us, has two connotations. On the one hand, empowerment, conveyed by the Latin root of the term itself (*possum,* meaning "I am able to"; in English, the same connotation can be glimpsed in the identity of form between the noun "might" and the verbal form "I might"); on the other hand, contingency and uncertainty: something that *may* happen *need not* happen. Making sure that it *does* happen is the business of action.

What resources does the subject invest in that business? Unfortunately most of what Simmel has to say on this topic is rather obscure (esp. 296; *230*). Some passages use the ancient distinction between the faculties of the will and of the intellect and superimpose it on the distinction between goals and means: the former express what we want and thus embody our will, whereas our intellectual capacities are chiefly involved in identifying the available means to those goals and choosing between them in the light of the ascertained "relationships and connections of reality" (591; *429*). The correspondence between will and goal-setting of course applies chiefly to what we may call ultimate goals, those sought entirely for their own sake and thus lying at the very end of means/goals chains; all other goals function instead as means to further goals, as intermediate links within means/goals chains, and to that extent turn into means (259–56; *208*). Since multiple, lengthy, and complex means/goals chains are characteristic of more advanced civilizations, in the latter men tend to develop their intellectual more than their volitional energies, there being many more means-posts, as it were, relative to goal posts, than under more primitive conditions. Thus advanced civilizations are generally associated with a predominance of intellectual concerns over as the pulsions of the self-positing will (592; *430*).

Taken at face value, this argument in *PdG* contrasts with another, according to which the will alights in the first instance on an "aspect of the world" which it turns into a goal, but subsequently becomes transferred to other aspects which function as means to that goal. But that transferral is itself an operation of the intellect, being dictated by the causal connections which the intellect perceives between the adoption of a given means or set of means and the goal sought for its own sake (591–92; *430*).

As to the motivations which lead people to act, Simmel disassociates himself from the view that they are always and necessarily of an egoistic nature. Interestingly, the alternative to egoism is constituted for him not only by altruism, but also by a third type of motivation. This consists in the subject's commitment to the matter at hand, in its dispassionate concern with the objective requirements and potentialities of whatever he/she is attending to. Individuals may comply with religious commandments, for instance, either for egoistic reasons—that is out of fear or hope as to what the divinity may do for/to them—or altruistically, out of sheer love of God. But, further, they may be motivated by their "feeling for the objective value of an ordering of the world within which the will of the highest principle finds unresisting expression in the will of all other elements" (309; *239*).

Nor is this motivational alternative a secondary or marginal one. According to Simmel, on the contrary, many complex collective undertakings function best when the participants are not directly inspired in their activities by their awareness of and commitment to the goal of the undertaking, but rather allow themselves to become absorbed in the demands of their own local roles, however circumscribed, seeking simply to do their best in them, and let the more distant results of their narrowly focused efforts take care of themselves (296ff.; *230ff.*).

Later we shall consider the notion of "objective spirit," which, as I see the matter, constitutes the ontological background to this motivational alternative to the dualism of egoism and altruism. Here, I shall just mention that, within the argument in *PdG* concerning the nature of action, that alternative comes closest to a very significant aspect of "the structure of social action" as Parsons construes it. According to Parsons the subjective ingredients of action always comprise a *normative* element: actors, that is, orient themselves to their circumstances and choose from possible courses of action in the light of both their direct interests and binding standards as to how they *ought* to conduct themselves—although they may violate rather than respect those standards. Parsons, however, connects with this view—derived, as he claims, by collating and analyzing the related insights of Weber, Durkheim, and others—a more elaborate understanding of action than can be derived directly from Simmel. For instance, there is no parallel in *PdG* to Parsons's emphasis on the standards of *symbolic appropriateness* which often control the conduct of actors.[9] Yet a passage of *PdG* strongly reminiscent of Sorel's statement quoted earlier clearly suggests the significance of the normative element of action in general:

> And indeed this is the formula of our whole existence, from the banal practice of everyday to the highest peak of intellectuality: in all our activity we have in front of us a norm, a criterion, an ideally preformed totality, which is carried over into the form of reality by means of that very activity. . . . A particular, more or less distinct feature of our acting can only be expressed by saying that through such acting, even when in terms of value it strongly violates the ideal, we accomplish a possibility which somehow preexisted it, an ideal program as it were. (634; *451*)

II

To move from the generic notion of action discussed so far to that of *economic* action, we must now consider in what ways subjects deal with the realm of objects. On one hand, Simmel suggests, "the ego would crumple up if it were not surrounded by external objects in which might find expression its tendencies, its energy and its peculiarities" (433; *323*). On the other, as we have repeatedly seen, the subject's very existence rests on its ability to distance itself from objects. According to Simmel, I suggest, the subject seeks to fulfill these contradictory tasks by means of a single activity that at the same time acknowledges the objects' existence and establishes the subject's mastery over them. The subject, that is, seeks to order objects, to arrange them according to criteria of the subject's own making.

Now, there are two basic ways in which which the subject can order objects: through *knowing* and through *valuing*. These two ordering activities are fundamentally distinct from one another, as Simmel argues at some length at the very beginning of *PdG*. The first expresses itself in judgments of fact, and yields the ordering of objects in the realm of Being, and particularly their causal connections. The second is manifested in judgments of value, that is, it places objects at some distance from one another on a scale of positive or negative significance that reflects the subject's commitment to a certain ideal of worth, to an Ought.

Although a stark contrast between Being and Ought (*Sein/Sollen*), judgment of fact and judgment of value, was commonplace in the Kant-inspired philosophical culture of Wilhelmine Germany, *PdG* takes the trouble to elaborate it somewhat. It warns the reader, for instance, against assuming that the dichotomy of knowing and valuing can be neatly subsumed under the dichotomy of objective and subjective. On one hand, both knowing and valuing are subjective activities through and through: as I indicated, both express themselves in judgments. On the other hand, they both emphatically refer to objects, and both in their different ways presuppose and foster the subject's distance from objects. However, they construe objects in radically different ways:

> Feelings about value have nothing to do with the structure of the things themselves. (293; *228*)

> As such, the object of volition is something other than the object of representation. Consider the analogy of love. The person we love is not at all the same reality which we cognitively represent to ourselves. . . . The marble of the Venus of Milo

means something quite different to the crystallographer and to the art critic. (52; 77)

At bottom, knowing is a matter of determining what is the case; and what is the case has always the same significance, or rather has no significance of its own, it is indifferent. Valuing is a matter of ranking, and as such aims at differences. We might say indeed that valuing establishes and generates those differences; yet in the valuing process we perceive ourselves as responding to dictates emanating from the objects themselves, which reflect their position on an inherent scale of value. (As somebody has remarked, when we express a judgment, say, about the aesthetic value of a painting, although we may acknowledge that it only expresses "the way we feel about it," if that judgment is challenged we do not look for confirmation within ourselves, we look—and point—at the painting.)

> The great categories [of being and value] share
> the feature of being fundamental, that is, the im-
> possibility of being reducible to one another or to
> simpler elements. (26; *61*)

> The reality of things, such as it confronts the
> spirit [*Geist*] in its purely cognitive capacity,
> knows nothing of values; in its indifferent unifor-
> mity, it operates in such a way that it often de-
> stroys what is most noble and spares what is
> most base, for it does not proceed according to
> hierarchies of worth, interest, or value. We then
> impose upon this natural, objective being a hier-
> archy of values, we divide it up according to what
> is good or evil, noble or low, precious or worth-
> less. This division in no way affects being itself in
> its tangible reality, yet being derives from it all

significance that it can have for us; and however clear we may be about the human origins of that division, we perceive it as having little to do with sheer fancy and arbitrariness. (180; *156–57*)

Different as they are, the activities of knowing and valuing are both continuous, necessary aspects of the subject's dealing with the world. These qualities need to be asserted particularly of valuing, because offhand a purely cognitive orientation to the world might appear primary and more indispensable: "Although our life appears determined by the mechanism and the objectivity of things, yet we cannot in reality move a step or have a thought unless our feelings invest things with values and orient to those our activity" (37; *84*). In fact, Simmel suggests, "even objective knowing proceeds from an evaluation" (25, *60*).

Thus knowing and valuing are both indispensable activities, yet they remain intrinsically different in nature; and, if we are to follow Simmel, we must assign our conceptual construction of economic action primarily to the sphere of valuing. This decision is somewhat surprising, since intuitively one would not consider economic action, given its "cool" and matter-of-fact nature, as being distinctively focused on value. Yet, although Simmel does not remark on this, the very term *value* has probably entered modern philosophical reflection from the discipline of economics in its classical phase.

We might say that in *PdG* Simmel unproblematically merges two meanings of *value*—the "hard" meaning derived from classical economics, including Marxism, and the "soft" meaning central to much late-nineteenth-century philosophical discourse, especially in Germany.

I say "unproblematically" because Simmel ignores some tensions that persist between the two meanings, as shown for instance by the fact that the expression *value*, and its equivalent in other languages, appears almost exclusively in its singular form when it carries the first meaning, and at least as often in the plural form (val-ue*s*, *Werte*, *valori*) when it carries the second.[10]

Furthermore, in Simmel the first meaning is largely subsumed under the second. Far from other values ap-pearing, in his thinking, as sublimated echoes of a pri-mordial economic value, economic value constitutes for him just one of a series of values, and is discussed initially as just one outcome of the generic valuing pro-cess. Unfortunately, although Simmel occasionally jux-taposes that outcome to a series of others—for exam-ple, "ethical, eudaemonistic, aesthetic, religious" values (180;*157*)—*PdG* never systematically discusses how they differ from and relate to one another. It is also unfortu-nate that sometimes Simmel's argument shifts too rap-idly, and perhaps inadvertently, from value in general to economic value in particular (e.g., 43; *72*).

In any case, what is involved in the valuing process in general? To begin with, as I have indicated, that process necessarily presupposes distancing: it cannot begin un-less there is a certain disengagement, a hiatus between the subject and the object of its own emotions: "In it-self, the object is not yet a value, as long as it is totally fused with the subjective process as the immediate stimulus to feelings, and constitutes as it were a self-standing component of our patrimony of feelings. It must become separated from this, in order to acquire the specific significance which we call value" (72; *89*). For the same reason, valuing is not associated with the attained possession of an object, the direct enjoyment of what it can offer the subject, or the sheer need for it or its consumption (in the case of economic activity) (72–73; *89–90*). It is associated, instead, with desiring (*Begehren*). This is a specific current of feeling which presupposes—and seeks to overcome—the distance (*Abstand*) between subject and object, but at the same time does not totally dominate and engross the subject: "The value of an object does indeed rest on its being desired, but only to the extent that the desiring has ceased to operate as a totally irresistible impulse" (43; *72*).

Thus, for Simmel, what invests the object with value is its desirability—a position which, incidentally, finds an echo in a classical anthropological definition of values as "conceptions of the desirable." Desirability in turn is associated with the fact that the object does not totally yield to the subject, but resists it, though not to the extent of becoming totally inaccessible. "This two-fold significance of desire, that it can arise only when there is a distance with respect to things which it seeks to overcome, yet it presupposes some proximity between the things and ourselves without which the existent distance could not be perceived, is conveyed by Plato's beautiful saying, that love constitutes an intermediate state between having and not having" (49; *76*). Thus, the valuing process has an objective aspect, in that desiring, the subjective activity which constitutes it, must, as it were, traverse a distance which at the same time confers subjectivity upon the subject and objectivity upon the object. But Simmel attributes to the process a further objective aspect, much harder to convey because, according to his construction of it, it transcends the difference itself between subjective and objective elements in the process. Although valuing expresses itself through a subject's judgment, that subject typically perceives its judgment as being called forth by the object itself, not (so to speak) as being graciously bestowed upon the object entirely on the subject's initiative. The subject's desire, instead, constitutes its response to an imperious claim for recognition emanating from the object. But that claim is grounded in turn in the object's relationship to an impersonal, self-standing realm of value, in its belonging to an intrinsically valuable category of things or thoughts.

This argument probably relates closely to one I reported previously concerning the tertium quid between egoism and altruism, and finds echoes in one I shall develop at greater length in a later chapter. In spite of these connections, I confess that I find it somewhat baffling; and for this reason, instead of trying further to elucidate it for the reader, I prefer to allow Simmel himself to make it at some length:

> Just as we represent certain statements as true while being at same time conscious that their truth does not depend on their being so represented, in the same way we feel, with respect to certain things, people, events, that they not only happen to be felt valuable by us, but would be valuable even if nobody estimated them. . . . Obviously this category lies beyond the controversy over the subjectivity or objectivity of value, because it dispenses with that relationship to a subject without which an "object" is no longer possible; it constitutes instead a third entity, of an ideal nature, which is inherent in that duality but not exhausted by it. On account of the practical

nature of its domain, the category establishes
a peculiar form of relationship to the subject,
which . . . can be described as a claim or request.
The value attaching to a given thing, person, or
event, *demands* to be acknowledged. As a fact, this
demand only manifests itself within us as subjects; yet as we yield to it we feel we are not simply satisfying a claim laid upon ourselves by ourselves—nor for that matter do we simply
acknowledge a quality of the object. . . . Considered purely from a naturalistic standpoint the
claim in question may appear subjective, whereas
from a subjective viewpoint it appears as something objective; in fact it constitutes a third category, not resulting from either of those two,
which lies as it were between ourselves and
things. . . . [It arises] from an ideal domain which
does not lie within us, nor does it purely adhere
as a quality of their own to the *objects* of valuation; rather it consists in the *significance* which
they acquire for us subjects by virtue of their location within the rankings of that ideal domain.
(36–38; *67–68*)

We need not fully accept (or indeed understand!) this
contention in order to grant to Simmel a more modest
one that I have already stated, to the effect that the valuing process, although it eventuates in the subject's
judgment, has objective aspects. Regrettably, as I have
already remarked, Simmel does not give us in *PdG* (or
in other writings that I know of) a taxonomy of value
forms or a systematic treatment of the related differences in the valuing process, indicating for instance
how those objective aspects vary, say, between the religious and the ethical value spheres. But on the whole

PdG conveys a view that one might phrase as follows: all values are objective, but some are more objective than others—not in the sense of having greater inter-subjective validity (although, as we shall see in a later chapter, this is the basic import of "objectivity" for Simmel) but in the sense that some value judgments require the subject to place a greater distance between itself and its own unreflected, raw emotional responses to the object, focusing its attention instead on the object itself.

Consider, for instance, Simmel's construction of the *aesthetic* valuing process—the only form of that process besides the economic form discussed at length in *PdG* (44–47; 75–77). According to him, the capacity for sustained, self-conscious aesthetic experience constituted a relatively late development in the course of the evolution of the human species. To experience "joy at the beauty of things" humans had to learn to sublimate earlier, more down-to-earth emotional responses to objects which caused them immediate sensual pleasure; and the specific element in that joy lies in "the consciousness of valuing and enjoying the *object* [*Sache*]," not in "a state of sensual . . . stimulation." (Remember, in *A Portrait of the Artist as a Young Man*, Stephen Daedalus's argument against the possibility of "kinetic art.") And "every cultivated male can in principle distinguish with assurance between the aesthetic and the sensual enjoyment of female beauty" (45; 76).

Another road to aesthetic experience originates not from men's immediate sensual response to stimulation, but from the practical utility some objects afford them. In the course of cultural development, according to Simmel, humans have learned to respond positively not (just) to the immediate *uses* of certain things in certain practical contexts but (also) to the sheer contemplation of those things' physical appearances, within or outside those contexts. This development may be replicated at the level of the individual: "While previously the object was valuable for us as a means to our practical or eudaemonistic ends, now it is its sheer visible form that causes our enjoyment, even as we stand before it in a more reserved, distant posture, without touching it." Or, its results at the level of the species are simply an acquired datum for later generations thanks to cultural transmission: "From the beginning, that has been beautiful for us which had previously proven useful to the species, and its perception affords us pleasure even when as individuals we do not have a concrete interest in this given object" (46; 77), which we are pleased simply to contemplate in the attitude Kant calls "aesthetic disinterestedness." Conceptually, in any case, what Simmel calls a "realistic pleasure" or a "concrete feeling toward things" needs to undergo a process of distancing, abstraction, or sublimation in order to become a properly "aesthetic feeling." And this process, Simmel insists, can also be seen as one of increasing "objectivation," for it makes the object's "quality and significance" depend less and less on the subject's "dispositions and needs."

So much for aesthetic experience; but what does this tell us about economic action, which revolves around a form of valuation very different from aesthetic valuation (44; 73)? In spite of that difference, Simmel treats the latter as an "analogy" to the former, because the two have much in common as concerns objectivation. They differ not so much in the length to which they take that process as in the way they do so. To phrase the matter briefly, aesthetic valuing objectivizes through sublimation; economic valuing objectivizes through comparison. Having briefly indicated above how Simmel makes the first point, I shall consider the second more closely.

Simmel's understanding of economic action, it seems to me, conveys a polemical intent. He seeks to counter both the man-in-the-street's identification of economic phenomena with those pertaining to the satisfaction of material needs and some of the more sophisticated alternative views—in particular, the view that the economy revolves around production and those which accord economic significance to whatever is scarce or has utility. For Simmel, as we shall see, the fundamental economic phenomenon is exchange, not production; and scarcity and utility, significant as they are, do not belong to the essence of that phenomenon. According to him, action is economic when it revolves around the comparison between two things (or states, or activities) each of which possesses value on its own terms, but in circumstances where the possession or fruition of both values by a given subject is not possible, and the possession or fruition of one must be surrendered in order to secure the possession or fruition of the other.

Exchange takes place, typically, when the two things (states or activities) in question are under the control of different individuals, each of whom surrenders what he/she controls in order to gain access to what is under the other's control; in these circumstances for exchange to take place means that the surrender is reciprocal. But in principle something like an exchange (and thus a primitive, Robinson Crusoe–like form of economic action) can be seen to take place when a given person considers different—and incompatible—uses of his/her own energies and resources and renounces some uses in order to secure others. One can construe as properly economic even an isolated man's decision to work in order to feed himself from the proceeds of work, insofar as he consciously renounces the benefits of leisure and undertakes the burden of labor in order to gain its benefits. Typically, however, an object acquires economic value insofar as somebody is willing to sacrifice control over another object in order to gain control over the former (64–65; *64*). "That a thing is worth something in purely economic terms, means that to me it is worth something, that is, that I am willing to give up *something* for it" (78; *92*).

Thus, the particular form of desire that activates economic action (as we have seen, according to Simmel all forms of action are activated by desire) not only—like other forms of desire—presupposes a certain distancing between subject and object, but furthermore undergoes the particular "cooling" effect of the question being posed, *which* objects of desire may be surrendered in order to gain *which other* objects of desire. To give an example, we remain within the realm of aesthetic valuing as long as we simply enjoy looking at paintings in an art gallery, or at those we already have at home; we step into the economic realm when we ask ourselves how many of our own Pissarros or Sisleys or Bonnards we are willing to barter against an art dealer's Monet. This imparts a particular abstractness (and a particular objectivity) to economic action: for the specific objects about which that question is raised no longer matter each in and of itself, but only in relation to one another. That abstractness is enhanced by the fact that typically economic value is quantitative: it reveals itself in *how much* of a given object of (preeconomic, so to speak) value is being surrendered in order to gain *how much* of another such object.

Alternatively, this could be phrased thus: economic value proper does not directly attach to things but, as it were, to the *ratio* between valued things. It is thus twice removed from the primary emotions directly awakened in men by things and once removed from the related values:

> Economic value emerges only by derivation
> from . . . primary, immediately experienced val-
> ues, insofar as their referents, by virtue of being
> exchangeable, are weighed against one another.
> But within this realm, no matter how constituted,
> economic value occupies with respect to the indi-
> vidual objects the same relationship which per-
> tains to value in general. It is a world apart, which
> partitions and ranks the concrete reality of ob-
> jects according to norms of its own, which do
> not lie in the objects themselves. By becoming
> ordered and arranged according to their
> economic values, things come to constitute a
> wholly different cosmos from that posited by
> their natural, immediate reality. (180–81; *157*)

Let me note in passing that economic phenomena can acquire such a degree of integration with one another, and of autonomy with respect to all other phenomena, only within a developed market system, and this pre-supposes in turn an advanced money system. These circumstances, however, allow full expression only to potentialities already inscribed, according to Simmel, in economic action per se, and which may find their primordial expression in a premonetary act of exchange, such as a barter.

The fact that economic action—like all action—is at bottom motivated by desire reveals itself, paradoxically, in the possibility of that desire finding expression through action other than economic: in particular, through the violent or deceitful *taking* of a desired object—through robbery, for instance. Here, the gaining of access to the desired object may be quite as deliberate as in exchange, but it is always a great deal more direct, less circuitous. Characteristically, robbery appears as a relatively frequent way of shifting objects between people only under "primitive" social and cultural circumstances, where people are less expected to control their feelings or to engage in sustained consideration of such abstract matters as the ratios between the values of things.

On this account, Simmel construes robbery (and its "altruistic" counterpart, gift-giving) as antithetical to economic action proper, in spite of the fact that robbery is a mode of acquisition and may be undertaken to meet consumption needs. One reason for so construing it is exactly that to Simmel robbery, like gift-giving, appears as an act highly laden with affect, highly "subjective." In contrast, as I have insisted, exchange is distinctively objective. (When Simmel offers his definition of man as "the objective animal," he suggests that it may be implied in Adam Smith's view of man as "the exchanging animal" [385;*291*].) Between robbery or gift-giving at one end and pure exchange at the other are ranged various intermediate forms—for instance, institutionalized gift-giving, with sanctioned expectations of reciprocity (85; *97*)—to which corresponds an increasing objective emphasis: "gift-giving comes to approximate a proper economy, capable of development, only when the toing-and-froing of things becomes objectified" (241; *195*).

As we have seen, in the typical act of exchange two individuals compare the values they attribute to two objects, of which each person controls one. As a result of this comparison, each of them surrenders one object only with the intent of gaining control over (or fruition of) the other, and thus only if and to the extent that he/she attributes to the other object greater value than he/she does to the first. Under these conditions, exchange has the significant property of loosening the hold of scarcity upon men, for it is not "zero-sum." That is, after each exchange act both parties have a greater sum of value at their disposal than before it (384; *290*). (Robbery, instead, is distinctively "zero-sum": the robber gains only to the extent than the victim loses.) Of course that property only holds as far as subjectively appraised values are concerned: "The more apt distribution brought about by exchange turns the objectively constant sum of values into a subjectively greater amount and higher measure of uses" (387; *292*).

Moreover, exchange is the culmination of a series of events, each of which must be construed not by considering a single term of reference but by considering the relations between more than one term. To begin with, all values rest on a judgment which places an object on a scale relative to other objects. Furthermore, as I have insisted, economic value in particular reflects a comparison between (at least) two primary values: "No matter how closely one scrutinizes a given object for those properties inherent in it, one cannot find its

economic value, for this consists exclusively in the reciprocal relation which those properties establish between
several objects, each of which conditions the other, and
reciprocates the significance which it receives from it"
(91–92; *101*). Furthermore, the typical exchange results
from the copresence and convergence of two such acts of
comparison, each carried out by a different individual.

Thus, economic value and exchange are distinctively
"relativistic" phenomena (93–94; *101–2*). This is what
Simmel intends to assert when he rejects all explana-
tions of the economic value of things which refer to such
properties as their utility, their scarcity, or the amount
of labor power necessary to produce them. The concept
of utility, to begin with, does not correctly designate
what determines economic value: "An object's utility as
such is not in a position to bring it into the economic
process unless it causes the object to be desired, which
does not always happen. . . . On the other hand, quite a
few things are desired by us, and economically valued,
which only an arbitrary stretching of linguistic practice
can designate as useful" (75; *91*).

The concept of scarcity has the advantage of being a
relative one; and, as we have already seen, exchange itself can be seen as a way of dealing with scarcity. Yet in
and of itself "the scarcity of goods would hardly cause
them to acquire value if we were not in a position to
modify it" either, again, through exchange, or through
productive labor—but, in its elementary form, labor itself can be construed as a matter of surrendering the
benefits of leisure for those of a larger stock of goods. In
any case, economic action does not flow unproblematically from the premises of either utility or scarcity: "For
if those premises were countered by people's ascetic re-

nunciation of useful or scarce objects, or if those premises were to eventuate merely in fighting or robbery—as
indeed often happens—then neither economic value nor
economic life would develop" (84; 96).

As to the Marxist view that the values of all objects
are grounded on the value of socially necessary labor
power objectified in them, Simmel objects that it does
not account for how labor power itself acquires value:
"It could hardly do so unless, by being exercised upon
various materials and by yielding various products, labor power had made exchange possible, or if the experience of labor had not been perceived as a sacrifice, undertaken for the sake of its outcome"—for, I repeat,
labor itself can be construed as involving an exchange,
be it (in the limiting, Robinson Crusoe–like case) between the courses of action open to a single individual
(84; 96).

Let us return briefly to the question I posed at the beginning of this section: what is the nature of economic
action? If I have reconstructed it correctly above, Simmel's answer can be summarized as follows. To begin
with, economic action emphatically shares a central
feature of all action, the reference to means and goals;
for conceptually it eventuates in the surrendering of one
value for the sake of another, and clearly the former
plays the role of means and the latter that of goal. Furthermore, the subjective processes orienting economic
action are typically quantitative in nature: they concern, in fact, *how much* to surrender of one value for
how much of another.

On these counts, we might say again that economic
action proper is generally carried out in a "cool," prevalently cognitive frame of mind, typically with a

considerable amount of purposeful deliberation. This is also the import of various previous considerations emphasizing the role which objects play within economic action, or the fact that such action presupposes a considerable distancing between the subject and its emotions. On the other hand, economic action results very much from *valuing* activities: it presupposes and compares values, and it revolves around a value form of its own. To phrase it in a less tender-minded fashion, economic action is very much *interested* action; its cognitive components are not, as it were, of a contemplative nature.

Unfortunately it is not very clear what empirical boundaries Simmel placed between this kind of action and others. He insists that economic action consists in exchange; and it might also seem as if for him, on the other hand, all exchange constitutes economic action. Yet this second point is more doubtful, for he expressly suggests that exchange can be considered as a model also for forms of interaction (say, in the sexual sphere) that he probably considered as intrinsically *non*economic (except, in that same sphere, for prostitution). Also, Simmel makes no attempt to chart conceptually the area broadly staked by his concept of economic action; he does not distinguish for instance, as Weber was to do, between economic action proper and *economically oriented action*, such as one undertaken on behalf of political goals but constrained by financial considerations.[11]

Simmel lacks—or does not seek—clarity on these matters for two reasons. First, he was keen to disassociate his own from traditional understandings of economic action (such as those emphasizing production, utility, or scarcity) that he considered too raw, and on that account he preferred not to anchor economic action in a materially distinctive, bounded region or phase of social existence. Second, it seems that Simmel did not much enjoy writing the first chapter of *PdG*, in which—in spite of the title, "Value and Money"—money plays a rather minor role, and in which he developed most of the insights I have sought to collate and relate in *this* chapter. It seems that his treatment of economic action was to him but a step toward his book's great, eponymous theme—money—and for this reason he dealt with the former theme in relatively sketchy fashion, as a conceptual way station toward a much more sustained, diverse, and original treatment of money.

We are now ready to follow him in that direction; but not before taking a short detour in the next chapter.

4

Objective Spirit

I

Simmel's reputation as a social theorist, particularly in English-speaking countries, rests largely on an understanding of his work that is correct and relevant, but—I submit—somewhat incomplete, for it pays insufficient attention to at least one significant aspect of his sociological work that is best represented in *Philosophie des Geldes*. Thus, in my view, one reason for making this work better known is to complement that understanding and leave us with a more comprehensive appreciation of Simmel's contribution.

Most contemporary students of social theory who are aware of Simmel's sociological work, refer to it in their writings, and make use of it in their own thinking do so primarily because Simmel affords numerous and valuable insights into what could be called the processual aspect of social reality. In this perspective, reality is produced and reproduced in the course and as a result of innumerable episodes of interaction between discrete units (individual and, less often, collective); and social theorizing is primarily concerned to identify under what conditions such episodes take place, how they evolve, and how they are terminated.

Simmel conceptualizes society itself not primarily as a structured entity, but as an ongoing, fluid process— Simmel calls it *Vergesellschaftung*, usually translated as "sociation"—driven forward by the participants' "reciprocal effects" (*Wechselwirkung*), by their coming together and apart. That process, he suggests, incessantly produces and reproduces structures, repetitive sets of outcomes and circumstances. For, as the participants come together and apart, unavoidably (and often inadvertently) they place themselves under certain constraints: for instance, those flowing from the fact that each interaction episode (or sequence of episodes) necessarily involves two, *or* three, *or* more parties.

This observation is more significant than it may at first appear. Often, for instance, the thoughts and activities of the participants in an interaction à trois (or more) are implicitly or explicitly affected by the possibility of the interaction in question surviving the departure or exclusion of one of the parties; whereas that possibility is out of the question when they interact à deux. Or, within a tryadic relationship of whatever nature, each party must consider—as a threat and/or as an opportunity—the possibility of forming an alliance with a second party to the disadvantage of the third; and the third party must select its strategies for limiting or subverting that disadvantage from a limited repertory of strategies which sociological analysis identifies. Also, the probability of certain forms of mutual attachment or hostility arising within a relationship may to an extent depend on the number of parties the relationship involves: consider, for instance, the pragmatic rule suggesting how many members of the Jesuit order their superior might send out together on an undertaking requiring their close, protracted cooperation: two never, four rarely, three as often as possible.

As I have already indicated, Simmel often suggested that the core task of sociology consists in exploring systematically these and similar ways in which the social process is constrained and affected by the very phenomenon it engenders—the development of more or less lasting, more or less extensive, more or less purposeful encounters and exchanges. Since those constraints often cut across the differences generated among those encounters and exchanges by their "content," that is, by the interests motivating and orienting the interacting parties, Simmel characterized the main concern of sociology as investigating instead the "forms" of interaction. His own essays on this theme produced brilliant insights, concerning for instance the unavoidable presence or possibility of conflict in all sustained interaction, no matter how benevolently motivated, or the extent to which mutually hostile or indifferent parties may be drawn together by the experience of shared conflict.

Although, as I suggested, Simmel practiced two other conceptions of sociology's task besides this "formal" one—those conceptions I labeled respectively *interstitial* and *molecular* in chapter 2—the first one has understandably shaped the received view of his distinctive contribution, stressing (I repeat) the processual nature of social reality, the significance of interactive effects, the flows of interaction from which one can abstract their "geometrical forms." Yet these conceptions of sociology—which do not, either singly or jointly, figure significantly in *Philosophie des Geldes*—leave unacknowledged Simmel's recurrent and imaginative concern with a different theme. The social process not only produces, and is controlled by, the invisible constraints deriving from the "geometry" of its occurrences; under certain conditions, the social process also eventuates in, and takes place by means and under the auspices of, man-made objects, of the visible, embodied products of past activity. As I have indicated in passing in the last chapter, objects are significant in human action not only as necessary counterparts to the emergence of subjects, but also as enduring outcomes of subjective activities, as public realities which subjects jointly experience and over which they contend, and which support, control, and frustrate their activities. But this perspective on social reality is not adequately acknowledged in the received view of Simmel's achievements, possibly because it is chiefly presupposed or expounded in his declaredly philosophical writings—and chiefly in *PdG* and in some late essays—rather than in his expressly sociological ones. In fact, the best conceptual avenue to this aspect of Simmel's contribution to social theory is constituted by an explicitly philosophical notion—that of "objective spirit" [*objektiver Geist*].

II

Before elaborating further the notion of objective spirit, and exploring its key manifestations in *PdG*, let us raise a question: how does this aspect of Simmel's social theorizing relate to his more sustained and express concern with the social process, with the flows of interaction? Unfortunately, *PdG* offers no clear answer to this query. In fact, the one passage which most expressly addresses it is somewhat obscure:

> Practical consciousness has found a form whereby the processes of relation and of reciprocal interaction through which reality advances become joined with the form of existence characteristic of substances, for even an abstract relation must clothe itself in such an existence. This ability to project mere relations into discrete aspects of reality is one of the great achievements of the spirit; for while it is true that in this way the spirit becomes embodied, it only does this in order to turn bodily reality into a vessel of spiritual reality, thus enabling it to operate in a fuller and more active way. (137; *129*)

Obscure as this statement may be, let us consider more closely the notion to which it refers, in order to identify its potential significance for social theory. So far as I know, the notion of objective spirit entered the philosophical vocabulary with Hegel. (Hegel's translators often prefer the term "objective *mind*.") In any case Simmel derived it (by way of two of his teachers at the University of Berlin, Lazarus and Steinthal)[1] from the Hegelian heritage in German philosophy, although it has been suggested that he did so almost unawares,[2] for his own philosophical roots lay much more in Kant's thought, and he belonged to the neo-Kantian generation in German philosophy, of which some have said that it no longer had any idea of what Hegel was all about.

In Hegel himself (to quote from a recent British *Dictionary of Philosophy*),

> spirit differs from nature in that spirit is an
> "I"; in Hegel's language, spirit has being "for it-
> self." Hegel recognizes three kinds of spirit: sub-
> jective, objective, absolute. The philosophy of
> *subjective spirit* studies the individual in abstrac-
> tion from his social relations, and discusses such
> topics as consciousness, memory, thought, and
> will. . . . The philosophy of *objective spirit* deals
> with a man's relations to his fellow man: the fun-
> damental concept here is that of "right" (*Recht*),
> a term having both a legal and a moral sense.
> This part of Hegel's philosophy includes his eth-
> ics and his political theory. The highest stage of
> spirit is *absolute spirit*, whose three parts are art,
> religion, and philosophy. . . . At this stage of
> thought, one realizes that subjective and objec-
> tive are one.[3]

In the way Simmel uses it, the notion of *objective spirit* comes close to being a philosophical formulation of the broad notion of *culture* characteristic of English, and then of American anthropology. The referent of that concept is the sum total of those enduring artifacts which it is given to humans not only to fashion for themselves, but to receive from others and to make available to others. And the following statement by Simmel shows how widely the two notions overlap:

> The objectification of the spirit constitutes the
> form which allows the preservation and accumu-
> lation of conscious labor. . . . Thus it turns into a
> historical fact something which is doubtful on a

biological basis: the inheritance of acquired characteristics. The advantage of man over other animals has been said to be, that he alone can be inheritor and not just descendant. But this distinction rests on that objectification of the spirit in words and works, organizations and traditions, which alone confers upon man his world—or indeed a world. (627; 453)

Why, then, not use *culture*, instead of the more mystifying notion of *objective spirit*, in our discussion of *PdG*? One reason is that Simmel himself uses *culture*, in that book and in other writings, in a different though related meaning (to be considered in chapter 7). A more important reason is that the Hegelian notion of *objective spirit* has philosophical overtones which remain significant for Simmel and suggest some significant aspects of the distinctive German approach to the social sciences mentioned in the first chapter. Let us consider some of these overtones, significant enough (I submit) to make *objective spirit*, in our context, a more appropriate expression than *culture*.

In the first place, the simple fact that in *objective spirit* the reference to culture (in the anthropological sense) is carried by an adjective (*objective*), suggests that culture is one manifestation among others of a wider phenomenon, indicated by the noun *spirit*. In Hegel's sequence, *subjective/objective/absolute*, the three terms of the sequence (though there is no parallel to *absolute spirit* in Simmel), clearly share an intrinsic affinity, since they constitute differentiated manifestations of the same reality. As Simmel writes in a later essay dealing with the relationship between the subject and the cultural object, *beide Parteien Geist sind*: both par ties are spirit. An important implication of this affinity is that cultural objects can have *meaning* for the subject—an important ontological premise of the so-called *Zirkel im Verstehen*, the "hermeneutical circle" formed by the interpreting subject and the interpreted object.[4]

A related implication of the adjective/noun relationship between *objective* and *spirit* is that the correspondence between them is never perfect; that the things in which the spirit objectifies itself never entirely exhaust the fullness of aspects and potentialities suggested by the notion itself of spirit. "For even when the spirit is bound up with materials, as it is in the case of tools, works of art, books, it never coincides entirely with what in such things can be perceived by the senses. It dwells in them in a . . . potential form, starting from which the individual conscience can actualize it" (626; *452*).

In Hegel, furthermore, *subjective* and *objective* are not simply juxtaposed as two adjectival manifestations of the same underlying reality: their succession also expresses, however obscurely, an underlying logic—conveyed by the notion of the *dialectic*—whose unfolding coincides with human history at large. (See the importance of the *pilgrimage* as a dialectical metaphor for historical development).[5] Simmel rejects this—indeed, any—philosophy of history: but not, as we shall see in a later chapter, the notion of dialectical development, particularly as applied to the individual subject.

Finally, the expression *objective* refers us also to the notion of *object*. It thus reminds us of the subject/object duality and the related tensions, while the notion of culture does not. Also, it suggests more clearly than *culture* does that the human products in question are generally sharply contoured and stubbornly structured; that they can be appropriated by other subjects than those who produce them; that they sometimes resist the will and frustrate the intent of the very subjects who produce them. In other terms, the "objective-ness" of cultural products is a premise, or perhaps an aspect, of the phenomenon of alienation.

Thus, the semantic freight of the notion of "objective spirit" is large and diverse—and, one may contend, somewhat murky. But so, I would counter, is the phenomenon to which it refers. At any rate, let us see what Simmel makes of it. To begin with—as I have already suggested—all manifestations of the objective spirit find their source in the interaction of individuals. "We can consider only the reciprocal activity between persons as the point of departure of all social formations [*aller sozialen Gestaltung*]. The actual beginnings of historical existence are wrapped in obscurity, but however they may have occurred, a genetic and systematic treatment must take off from this simplest and most immediate relationship, which we still find at the origins of innumerable new social formations" (208; *174*). This view is less uncontentious than it seems; for, as Simmel makes clear, it prohibits considering the larger social institutions—such as "language, morality, law, religion"—as the inventions of single individuals. Even when these play a major role in their genesis, they do so only in interaction with larger numbers of them (88–89; *58*).

By the same token, typically the constituent aspects of the objective spirit are interindividually accessible, available; they constitute, as I said, public realities. Many individuals can make use of, at any rate, certain *kinds* of cultural products (unfortunately Simmel does not specify conceptually which kinds, but contents himself with exemplifying them: "books, art, ideal concepts such as fatherland . . . the knowledge of a thousand interesting and significant things" [386; *291*]) without taking them away from one another, without competing for them. Furthermore, cultural products typically *bind time*, because they remain available after the activity of producing them has terminated and often endure after the disappearance of the subjects themselves of those activities. Hence the tendency for the stock of cultural products to build up over time—a tendency which has visibly accelerated, Simmel notices, in the nineteenth century (621; *449*).

Finally, although the whole realm of the objective spirit is in a sense a means to the end of human survival, an extension of man's freedom, its components are not indefinitely responsive to human purposes, infinitely pliable. "Our freedom finds its limit in the given object's properties. . . . For only to the extent that an object is something for itself, can it be something for us; thus, only insofar as it sets boundaries to our freedom, does it make room for it" (435–36; *324–25*).

These general considerations about the objective spirit are not complemented in *PdG* (or, so far as I know, in other writings of Simmel's) by anything resembling a typology of its manifestations or a systematic discussion of the constituent parts of such a typology. Before drawing on Hans Freyer for this kind of treatment, we may assemble into a brief but not insignificant argument what *PdG* has to say about "(social) institutions." These constitute the most significant manifestations of the objective spirit, at any rate for social theory; besides, it is under the concept of institution that money itself can be classified. Another reason for us to pay special attention to that concept is that it was to have a significant career in later German social theory, and particularly in the work of Arnold Gehlen.

As is generally the case in the German sociological tradition, *PdG* conceptualizes institutions not as groupings, "manned" collective entities such as a party or a church, but as rather more abstract phenomena. They are broad complexes of rules, arrangements, resources, and bodies of personnel, which attend to distinctive, critical human concerns, comprehensively characterized in *PdG* as "values": religious values, ethical, political, and so on.

Consistently with his general views on the objective spirit, Simmel contends that institutions, too, originate from the spontaneous practices of interacting individuals. But

> further development replaces this immediacy
> of the mutually affecting forces by constituting
> superpersonal formations, which appear as self-
> standing representatives of those forces, and
> which take upon themselves and mediate the re-
> lations of individuals with one another. . . . Thus,
> from the requirements and arrangements which
> at first emerge in the traffic among group associ-
> ates, and which eventually become fixated, there
> emerged the objective laws of custom, law, and
> morals. They are ideal products of the human ca-
> pacity to represent and to evaluate, which at this
> point exist for our thought wholly beyond the in-
> dividual's will and activity, as (so to speak) their
> "pure forms." (208–9; *174*)

Once developed, institutions present themselves to individuals as established, public realities, often given visible, commanding form by collective entities, with distinctive material resources, physical locales, privileges, and status systems: for instance, "religious value embodies itself in priests and churches, ethical and social values in the officials and the visible institutions of state power. . . . The money economy becomes crystallized into the self-standing structure of the stock market, in the same way that political organization becomes crystallized in the state."

This process of structure-building not only maps differentiated sets of arrangements onto the surface of the larger society; it is also carried on within each set. For instance, state power becomes divided between relatively different establishments, from the judiciary to the army, each with resources and practices of its own; in a political party an executive elected more or less directly by the rank and file stands over against the parliamentary group, which has a constituency of its own in the party electorate.

All this has two contrasting effects for the individual. On the one hand,

> by making use of social institutions, individuals
> can attain goals which would never have been
> within their reach otherwise. Leaving aside the
> most general effect—that the participation in
> the state constitutes for them, via the physical
> protection it offers, the premise of most goal-
> oriented activities—the special institutions of
> private law opens to the will of individuals possi-
> bilities of affirmation which otherwise would
> have been wholly denied to them. Insofar as an
> individual's will is routed through the legal ave-
> nues of contract, testament, adoption, etc., the

individual avails itself of an instrument arranged
by the generality, and which multiplies its own
energy, extending its reach, securing its outcomes.
(262; *209*)

On the other hand, institutions operate as constraints
upon the individuals, by setting targets for them, standards for their activities: "the activities of the artist,
the civil servant, the preacher, the teacher, the researcher must be measured, in their factual content,
against an objective standard, and only to the extent
that they meet it do they afford subjective satisfaction
to their protagonist" (416; *311*).

These two effects are closely related; for it is only by
disciplining and sanctioning the activities of each individual that an institution can constitute "a central station for innumerable teleological itineraries (*Kurven*) of
a number of individuals" (416; *311*), and operate as a
dense concentration of social power. In the modern
state, for instance, thanks only to the centralization of
administrative power into the bureaucracy, "the energies of society are brought together in such concentrated form, that it can confront any contingency and
achieve maximum performance with a minimum of expended energy" (244–45; *197*).

By the same token, however, institutions may become
the loci of relatively self-standing interests, deploy the
power built into them more and more on their own behalf, and stand less and less at the service of the social
values they are supposed to foster, including their ability to guide and support the individual's pursuits. It
thus becomes difficult to determine, at times, whether
an institution is operating as a specialized part of a

larger whole, or as if it constituted, itself, a self-standing whole. Again using the state as an example: "Certainly its significance lies in standing above the parties and their interests, and it is to this abstract superiority that it owes its power, its unimpeachability, its position as the highest agency of society. Yet, once it has acquired those properties, it often intervenes in the struggle among sectional social forces, and takes the side of one of these against the others, so that these, while comprised within the state in its wider sense, confront it in its narrower sense as one power confronts another" (692–93; *496*). As we shall see in chapter 7, this line of argument merges with a number of others in a sustained, pathos-laden argument about the phenomenon of alienation.

III

Simmel's use of the concept of objective spirit, while fragmentary (in *PdG* as well as in other writings) constitutes a significant episode in a prolonged exploration of that concept within German social theory—an exploration that begins with Hegel and culminates in the work of Arnold Gehlen. A significant link between Simmel's thinking on these matters and Gehlen's own (focused, as I have mentioned, on the notion of institution)[6] is constituted by the work of the philosopher and social theorist Hans Freyer, and particularly by his *Theorie des objektiven Geistes* (1923).

I report some parts of Freyer's argument in that book not so much with the intent of reconstructing a sequence in intellectual history as because Freyer offers a fairly systematic analysis of the concept of objective spirit and thus neatly complements Simmel's own argument, which never bothers to systematize its many insights.

First, a few words about an author who was very poorly known in English speaking countries until, a few years ago, he became the subject of a substantial intellectual biography.[7] Hans Freyer was born in 1887 and taught philosophy and sociology between the wars in Kiel and Leipzig (where Arnold Gehlen was among his students), and subsequently in Budapest. Prominent among the right-wing intellectual opponents of the Weimar republic as a critic of modern, Western values and institutions, during the Third Reich he became a significant figure in the academic establishment. Set aside at first during the process of denazification after World War II, he held an important editorial post in publishing, but he then returned to academic work at the University of Münster. Although Freyer's standing in postwar German sociology was damaged by the evidence of how seriously Freyer had compromised himself with the Nazi regime, he never recanted his intellectual positions, which had affinities with the Nazi ideology but could not be identified with it. He died in 1969, leaving behind a significant body of work: besides *Theorie des objektiven Geistes*, his most important writings were *Soziologie als Wirklichkeitswissenschaft* (1930), *Weltgeschichte Europas* (1947), and *Theorie des gegenwärtiges Zeitalters* (1955).

Theorie des objektiven Geistes, which bears the subtitle "An Introduction to the Philosophy of Culture," offers a brief, limpid discussion of the nature of the "cultural/historical world," explicitly conceptualized as "objective spirit." I draw almost exclusively on its first chapter, "The Objective Spirit as Being." (Chapters 2 and 3 view it instead "as process" and "as system.")

The reader may remember that early on in this book I quoted from *Theorie des objektiven Geistes* a eulogy of German *Historismus*, a passage where Freyer praises that tradition for identifying in *Verstehen* (sympathetic understanding) the sole avenue to a correct appreciation of cultural achievements and historical events. This hermeneutical emphasis—which makes the book a significant entry in the vast German literature dealing with hermeneutics—shows also in Freyer's construction of the genesis of the objective spirit. For the threefold process of "objectivation" which, as we shall see, eventuates in the objective spirit, starts from an elementary communicative activity: a gesture (*Gebärde*) such as pointing.

Unlike the activity, say, of balling a fist, or striking a table, in anger, "the pointing gesture of the stretched finger . . . does not find its meaning (*Sinn*) in the fact of its expressing a psychical process" but in the fact of its designating a part of the external world. To that extent, it presupposes and expresses a basic assumption about the world that Freyer (following Dilthey) calls "objective conception" (*gegenständliche Auffassung*). It also constitutes the "first objectivation," that is, a differentiation between the pointing subject and the object pointed at, which according to Freyer makes it possible for subjects to assume a "theoretical" posture toward the world. "The phenomenological presupposition of such a sign is that the objective world has separated itself from the totality of experience and constitutes a coherent complex [*Zusammenhang*], between parts of which real relations obtain."

The "second objectivation" results from the following consideration: the meaning of the gesture in question is indifferent to the variations in the pointing activity. Different people in different situations will point to the same object in different ways; yet "however it is performed, the gesture still means: the book is there." In the same way that for most purposes, within a given painting, it does not matter whether the painter has used first the red and then the blue, or whether seconds or years have lapsed between individual brushstrokes, "in the designating gesture the sign emancipates itself from the process of its genesis, becomes crystallized, becomes . . . the objective carrier of an objective meaning. . . . The gesture designates something objective within the objective world in an objective fashion."

Finally, we are witnessing a "third objectivation" insofar as an activity of this kind *embodies itself*, ceases to coincide entirely with its execution, becomes an enduring aspect of external reality. Hannah Arendt has made a similar point as follows: "Action, speech and thought . . . in themselves do not 'produce,' bring forth anything. . . . In order to become worldly things, that is, deeds and facts and events and patterns of thought and ideas, they must first be seen, heard and remembered," and to that end they must be "transformed, reified as it were, into things—into the sayings of poetry, the written page or the printed book, into paintings and sculptures, into all sorts of records, documents and monuments."[8]

As Freyer suggests, only what has gone through all three "objectivations" comes to be part of the objective spirit; thus, for instance, the pointing gesture does not, the road sign does. I shall translate somewhat liberally a lengthy passage that makes this point:

> Drawing our examples from the experience of primitive peoples, consider objects giving the following indications: "Here lie the boundaries of the tribe," "Here a body is buried," "This pertains to the chieftain," "The fruits of this field are taboo." The signs which have these meanings constitute objective spirit in that they represent all three objectifications. In the first place, their significance is objective: their meaning is not a psychical experience, but an objective state of things. In the second place, wherever they find themselves, they carry their own meanings in themselves, they have let themselves loose from their genetic process; I understand their meaning without knowing anything about how they came to be or without interpreting them psychologically. In the third place, they are not meaningful acts, but material things; they have embodied themselves and become autonomous with respect to the living beings who brought them about; they endure over and beyond the duration of the acts which brought them about.

To emphasize that the cultural product has transcended the act of producing it, Freyer has recourse to the notion of "form": "For a meaningful spiritual content to become form, means that it has let itself loose from the acts in which it lives, it has acquired an existence that transcends experience, no matter whether it did so by becoming materially embodied, or in the more elevated form of a principle or norm which commands actual experience to follow its own dictates."

This last passage suggests that the objective spirit is a realm comprising very different constituents. A section of the chapter from *Theorie des objektiven Geistes* under examination here (55–74) develops this point. It first remarks that most manifestations of the objective spirit appear grouped into diverse, self-standing clusters, which Freyer calls "worlds": the world of religions, that of law, that of art, and so on.

However, Freyer emphasizes another kind of differentiation, which he treats as corresponding to the "chief directions in which the third objectivation can take place." In so doing he offers what, as I have remarked, Simmel conspicuously refuses to offer, a typology of the objective spirit. This typology, as Freyer construes it, has five components; I give below the respective German labels, because it is not always clear to me how they ought to be translated into English:

1. *Gebilde* (structure?). Freyer calls an objective form a *Gebilde* "when its meaning content does not refer to another meaning content, but stands by itself, although it does relate to the outside world. The purest example . . . is a work of art." Other examples are scientific concepts, religious systems, and political orders.

2. *Gerät* (device?). These manifestations of the objective spirit, in contrast, intrinsically point beyond themselves, for they make sense only as intervening components of (to use Simmel's language) teleological, means/goals series.

3. *Zeichen* (sign?). Again, such a form of the objective spirit points to beyond itself, but mainly by referring to other aspects of reality, rather than by actively impinging on them (as *Geräte* do). However,

Freyer characterizes the *Zeichen* primarily by contrasting it with the prime example of a *Gebilde*, the work of art. Like the *Zeichen*, "the work of art also has a meaningful content, but the point of it is not to refer via that content to something objective. . . . It would not make sense to say that the pictorial nude refers to the model. A sepulchral effigy, on the contrary, does intend to refer to something, and this is what makes it a *Zeichen*, whether or not besides that it also is artistically significant. In the same way, a devotional holy image . . . functions in the first place not as a *Gebilde* but as a *Zeichen*."

4. *Sozialform* (social formation?). Freyer construes in a manner highly reminiscent of Simmel's concept of institution the fact that over time multiple episodes of interindividual interaction focused on some shared concern condense into standardized arrangements, yield patterns which in the long run will inspire and regulate the very activities and feelings from which originally they sprang—until "there comes into being a social organism whose specific forms persist even as individuals enter it or abandon it." The elementary manifestation of this phenomenon is a given "social rule"; but such rules can become components of gigantic complexes of rules, capable of enduring for centuries.

Freyer construes this phenomenon in a way which has organicist overtones, probably directed against Weber's resolutely individualistic construction of social aggregates:

Obviously such formations depend at any given time on the fugitive acts whereby they are enacted; and one may be tempted to resolve, for instance, the reality of the state wholly into specific acts of command, obedience, participation, fiscal compliance, into specific experienced feelings, such as a feeling of reassurance or of patriotic enthusiasm. Yet this would exhaustively analyze the reality of the state just as little as the reality of a work of art would be exhausted by analyzing the psychological processes involved in producing it or contemplating it. In both cases, something remains that transcends the acts: an objective form with a specific meaning content.

What distinguishes a *Sozialform* from a *Gerät* is the fact that the latter is much more narrowly focused on a specific purpose. There is greater similarity between *Sozialformen* and *Gebilde:* "Social formations appear to be nothing else but *Gebilde* constituted by living human beings. It comes natural to us to think of the state as a work of art, or of the family as a natural *Gebilde*"— although the former "are not erected as buildings are, rather performed as musical compositions are."

5. *Bildung.* There really is not a good translation for this term, for as Freyer uses it here it points to something rather obscure, which in any case stands at the very margin of the realm of objective spirit. According to one of Freyer's statements, the referent of *Bildung* is constituted by certain modes and aspects of activity, certain muscular and intellectual dispositions, which over time become built into the unreflected practices of individuals—for instance, into the way an artisan holds a tool, or the ability to decide at a glance how much effort to exercise while using the tool on a given piece of material. Yet according to another statement, what is involved in *Bildung* "is not so much acts, or a series of acts, or dispositions to act, but ulti-

mately the person itself which lies before and under all active life."

Thus understood, the notion of *Bildung* primarily conveys the German ideal of the *gebildete Person*, the aesthetically sensitive, thoroughly cultured individual, who is familiar in particular with the canon of great European literature and who can, to use an expression of Goethe's, "give himself an account of the last two thousand years of history"; and this is an ideal Simmel himself shared. But Simmel, as we shall see, saw at least a potential contrast between that ideal and the realm of the objective spirit, at any rate in its overly massive, differentiated and seductive modern embodiments. As to Freyer, it is not at all clear to me why he saw fit to add that notion of *Bildung* to his own elaboration of the concept of objective spirit.

IV

I have indicated that both Simmel and Freyer write within the German tradition originating in Hegel; and some tough-minded readers may feel that this legacy somehow invalidates their arguments about the objective spirit by tying them closely to the redoubtable metaphysical assumptions and cognitive strategies of idealism, of which such readers caught a disturbing glimpse in my earlier quote about Hegel's "system of the spirit." Yet one may derive some support for Simmel's insights (and indirectly for Freyer's) from surprising quarters—in particular from recent writings of Karl Popper, a twentieth-century philosopher whose reputation in the English-speaking world was originally founded, paradoxically, on his sharp criticism of Hegel.[9]

So far as I can see, in the current philosophical scene Popper stands as the very embodiment of what one may call sophisticated common sense. His work on the philosophy of science (including social science) has advanced a position sometimes called "critical rationalism," which opposes any form of system-building, especially the kind that draws inspiration from "dialectical" notions of "totality," and urges the significance, nay, the necessity, of a strategic appeal to empirical evidence in the construction of theory.

Yet two essays Popper wrote in the 1960s, "Epistemology without a Knowing Subject," and "On the Theory of the Objective Mind" (where "mind" stands as a translation of *Geist* alternative to "spirit") put forward views which strongly remind one of some of Simmel's arguments.[10] I refer in particular to Simmel's view (echoed to an extent by Freyer) that the human products which constitute the objective spirit comprise not only materially embodied artifacts and institutional arrangements, but also purely intellectual constructions, for instance complexes of rules or of logical statements. Popper attains a similar result (I suggest)[11] in his argument to the effect that an exhaustive ontology must accommodate three distinct realms of being, which he labels the "three worlds": "First, the world of physical objects and physical states; secondly, the world of states of consciousness, or of mental states, or perhaps of behavioral dispositions to act; and thirdly, the world of objective contents of thought, especially of scientific and poetic thoughts and of works of art" (106). Among the "inmates" of this world (or World Three, as he sometimes labels it) Popper cites "theoretical systems; the state of a discussion or the state of a critical argument; and, of course, the contents of journals, books, and libraries" (107). In a later essay he states: "The third world is the world of intelligibles, or of ideas in the objective sense; it is the world of possible objects or thought; the world of theories in themselves and of their logical relations; of arguments in themselves; and of problem situations in themselves" (154).

Let me emphasize what a strong claim this is. Among the components of this third world, it seems, are not only, say, those theorems that have been stated and proved with reference to a given set of axioms, but also those theorems implicitly generated by stating the axioms but which have not yet been stated, let alone proved. For Popper such items do not owe their existence exclusively to the fact that they are mental representations entertained by individuals; this would make them part of the "second world," whereas they possess, he claims, "independent existence."

In both the essays I have referred to, Popper concentrates on the epistemological aspects of the distinction between the "three worlds" and more specifically of the existence of the third. But he also argues "three supporting theses: the first of these is that the third world is a natural product of the human mind, comparable to a spider's web. The second . . . is that the third world is largely *autonomous*, even though we constantly act upon it and are acted upon by it. . . . The third . . . is that it is through interaction between ourselves and the third world that objective knowledge grows" (112).

One aspect of the claimed *autonomy* of the third world is that its denizens, once constituted through the actions of men, develop aspects and relations of their own making. For instance, "the sequence of natural numbers is a human construction. But . . . it creates its own autonomous problems in its turn. The distinction between odd and even numbers is not created by us: it is an unintended and unavoidable consequence of our creation. Prime numbers, of course, are similarly unintended autonomous and objective facts" which human subjects can make into the theme of their inquiries. Something similar, Popper argues, applies to artistic experience. This, at any rate in its creative moments, amounts to the solution of problems which are autonomously generated by "the state of the art." He quotes Gombrich's claim that "the artist works like the scientist. His works exist not only for their own sake but also to demonstrate certain problem-solutions" (180).

These arguments, I think, find fairly close correspondence in some developed by Simmel in *PdG*, and which according to him demonstrate the validity of Plato's doctrine postulating a realm of ideal essences which human knowledge can at best approximate. Such correspondence between Simmel and Popper is ironic, considering that Plato shares with Hegel the privilege of having served as a prime target in *The Open Society and Its Enemies*, the work that originally established Popper's high scholarly standing in the English-speaking world. In any case, Simmel draws on Plato when he argues that some phenomena in the realm of the objective spirit can only be understood by assuming "that there is an ideal domain of theoretical values, of perfect intellectual significance and coherence, which coincides neither with objects—for indeed these are only its objects—nor with the amount of knowledge which at any given time has been attained and is psychologically available. Such knowledge, in fact, always little by little, and partially, achieves agreement with that which comprises all possible truth, and shares in that truth to the extent that it does so agree" (623; *450*). For example:

> If it is legitimate to say that the law of gravity was valid before Newton stated it, then the law itself does not dwell in the concretely given masses of matter. It only signifies the manner in which the relations between those matters represent themselves in a given mind, and its validity does not depend on their being matter in reality. By the same token the law dwells neither in objective things, nor in the subjective minds, but rather in that sphere of the objective spirit from which our capacity for truth absorbs one aspect after another. Once Newton had done this with respect to the law in question, it became incorporated into the historical objective spirit, and at this point its ideal significance within that spirit no longer depends on its being echoed within a given individual. (626–27; *452*)

As I read it, this view suggests one aspect, relevant to cognitive activity, of the intrinsic *normativity* of human action, a notion I introduced in chapter 3 while acknowledging that it is not conspicuously present in *PdG*. In the same way that for Simmel all practical action always represents an approximation to something perceived as valuable, all cognitive action is intrinsically oriented to a preexistent realm of truth. As I have recognized, in *The Structure of Social Action* Parsons rightly gives much more emphasis to this aspect of action than it receives from Simmel's less sustained and self-conscious exploration of the action concept. Parsons, on the other hand, misses the dialectical relationship the notion of objective spirit posits between subject and object. For in Simmel (though not in Plato) the ideal realm where all truth and all value ultimately reside, and whence they set norms for all human practical and cognitive striving, is itself the product of subjective activity: it is, as I have suggested, another *adjectival* manifestation of the same underlying *substance*, the spirit itself. In that sense all norms are ultimately self-imposed, all constraints upon freedom derive from earlier expressions of freedom and set targets for later expressions.

Goethe gives a clever example of this relationship in one of the most remarkable exchanges in *Faust*, when Faust for the first time confronts Mephistopheles, whom he had encountered disguised as a stray dog during a walk, and whom he had taken back to his study. When Mephistopheles reveals himself, this time as a wandering scholar, Faust asks him why previously, while Faust was reading from and translating the Holy Scriptures, thus causing the dog great distress, Mephistopheles had not let himself out of the study. He could not make an exit, Mephistopheles answers, because, by pure chance, a forbidding magical sign had interposed itself between the dog and the door. Why then not exit through the window? Faust asks. That was also out of the question, Mephistopheles explains. For

> It is a law with devils and with spirits—
> Whichever way they let themselves in, there
> also they must exit.
> In the first we are free; in the second we are
> slaves.[12]

As this suggests, and as I shall insist in the last chapter, the fact that the subject and the object are two expres-

sions of the same reality, the former expressing and re-
alizing itself in the second, has a twofold significance.
On the one hand, to quote Simmel again, *beide Parteien
Geist sind,* and on that account the subject can gain and
grow from its access to the object. On the other hand,
the object can also constrain the subject, hinder its
search for self-realization, and frustrate it. This, I repeat, is the most significant insight to be drawn from
the notion of objective spirit and the related dialectical
imagery in *Philosophie des Geldes.*

5

Money: Its Properties and Effects

In chapter 3 I indicated how Simmel conceptualizes economic action; and in chapter 4 I laid some emphasis on his notion of (social) institution. Unfortunately, *Philosophie des Geldes* does not expressly bring these two themes to bear on one another. That is, it offers no systematic discussion of the chief institutions that subserve and control economic life but devotes only occasional attention to property, the market, contract, and the enterprise. The great exception among the institutions of economic life is money, for *this* of course is what the book is all about.

Perhaps to stress his resolute avoidance of technical economic matters, Simmel does not offer a formal definition of money; he prefers to rely on his reader's ordinary understanding of its nature. But he expressly conceptualizes money as an institution (e.g., 454; 397), and most of his book deals with a number of significant questions one can raise about that institution within the framework of social theory. What is the significance of money for social life at large, and for modern social life in particular? What is required for money to exist, how does it function, and what proximate and remote effects does it have on the way people act and think? What other developments in social life at large are associated with the development of money?

My own treatment of these questions will of course be much more succinct than Simmel's own; it will also be more selective. It is focused specifically on money as an institution, and on other institutional phenomena associated with it, and mostly ignores the many and remarkably insightful arguments of Simmel's concerning the sociopsychological aspects of the money phenomenon. On the other hand, my treatment seeks to be more systematic than Simmel's. I distinguish more sharply than he does the following themes:

how should we conceive of money's nature and of its essential functions?

what basic properties allow money to perform those functions?

what other institutions must exist for money itself to come into being and develop? Conversely,

with what other institutions does money have an intrinsic affinity?

what have been the major stages in the institutional development of money?

This book raises all these questions within a single chapter, and thus may convey a distorted image of the contents of *PdG*, for it does not reflect the absolutely prominent place the money phenomenon occupies in that whole book. This is of course one more reason for my readers to engage in their own dialogue with Simmel's text.

I.   What Is Money?

We saw in chapter 3 that the essence of economic action lies in exchange. Objects acquire economic value insofar as they are not considered each in itself but rather compared with one another to determine what other object each can be exchanged for. Money, in turn, exists primarily to facilitate such comparisons and to mediate the resulting exchanges; "It is, so to speak, the interchangeability [*Fungibilität*] of things personified" (128; *124*), and on this account money constitutes "the general concept of things insofar as they are economic" (715; *511*). In particular, the price attaching to a commodity in a developed money economy expresses its value in relation to other commodities, and nothing else: not, at any rate, anything intrinsic to a given commodity in itself, which is the supposed referent of the "just price" often authoritatively assigned an object in an underdeveloped money economy (132; *126*):

> The value which attaches to things on account
> of their exchangeability, this metamorphosis
> of their value through which it becomes eco-
> nomic, comes more openly and powerfully to the
> fore in things as the economy gains scope and
> intensity. . . . But only money, by its very essence,
> gives this development its utmost expression,
> [for] it is nothing but the pure form of exchange-
> ability, it embodies that aspect or function which
> makes things economic, and which is not all
> there is to things, but *is* all there is to money
> itself. (138; *130;* my emphasis)

In fact, money not only imparts evidence to that interchangeability which confers on things their economic value but expresses a very general property of experience—"that things attain their meaning from one another, and that their being and their determinate configuration [*Sein und Sosein*] are constituted by the mutual relations on which they rest" (136; *128–29*).

As we noted in chapter 3, in principle the comparisons that establish the economic significance of objects, leading to the surrender of one for the acquisition of another, need not involve more than one actor; even an isolated actor—like Robinson Crusoe—may engage in such comparisons between his own leisure and his own labor, or between different kinds of laboring activity open to himself. This solipsistic form of economic conduct is out of the question with money, which constitutes "an exclusively sociological form, wholly meaningless with reference to a single individual" (189; *163*). "In brief, money is the expression and the instrument of a relationship, of men's mutual dependency, of their relativity, which makes the satisfaction of one's desires depend on another, and vice versa" (179; *156*).

While, as I indicated, Simmel does not formally define money, the closest he comes to a purely conceptual presentation of it is a passage which considers it as a link, an element intervening in interindividual exchanges. Given a situation involving two parties A and B, if A wants an object *b* which B has, but cannot induce him to hand over *b* because B does not want that *a* which A can supply, it is useful for some X to exist into which A can convert *a* at any time and which B can be assumed to want, because he can exchange it in turn for any *c*, *d*, or *e* he may want from C, D, or E. For under these circumstances A can use some amount of the X in his control in order to acquire *b* from B, who in due course can decide into what to convert that amount of X (263; *210*).

Whatever functions as X in this example constitutes money; and the point of money's existence is ultimately to convey, by being expended and received, the individuals' valuations of objects intrinsically apt to satisfy their desires, while money itself cannot do this directly, for money possesses no value of its own (197; *168*). But money expresses and represents those valuations in a uniquely effective manner; and in this critical capacity (245; *198*) are grounded all of money's functions: both the primary one (acting as a means of exchange) and the derivative ones, such as "storing and transferring value" and "measuring" it (179; *156*). Its capacity to express and represent valuations, furthermore, indicates that money is at bottom a symbolic phenomenon, sharing with other symbols the uniquely human ability to let something *stand for* something else (162–66; *146–49*).

II. Properties of Money

Money can perform various exchange functions because, and to the extent that, it has some distinctive properties. Once more, Simmel is hardly systematic in his treatment of those properties, which furthermore is at times somewhat diffuse. This second aspect of his treatment is easier to improve on, simply by being succinct; as to the first, I try to systematize somewhat Simmel's treatment by grouping most of the properties he mentions into a much smaller number of what I call "conceptual clusters," that is, sets of closely associated qualities. I try to design the clusters so as to maximize the overlap between the properties within each and minimize the overlap between the clusters themselves; but this second condition is less easy to satisfy than the first.

My first conceptual cluster concerns what I would call the "instrumentality" of money; or, to use Simmel's own wording, the fact that "money is the purest form of the tool" (263; *210*). What Simmel here means by "tool" (*Werkzeug*) can be indicated generically by conceiving of it as a particular manifestation of the objective spirit (as with Freyer's *Geräte*, see chapter 4), and, more specifically, with a quote from *PdG:* "On the one hand [the tool] is an external object which operates mechanically, on the other it is also something we operate not merely *upon* but also *with.* . . . The tool is an intensified instrument, for its form and existence are determined by the goal (of action). . . . It is not itself a goal" (261; *209*). Of course one may qualify money as a tool only in a rather metaphorical sense; more appropriately, one may designate it as belonging (as I have already suggested) in a rather special, and sophisticated, category of tools, the "social institution" (262; *209*). But again among institutions money is distinguished by its strongly instrumental nature, already suggested by the previous account of how it intervenes in facilitating exchanges, to the effect that "what money in its totality mediates is not the possession of objects, rather their exchange for one another" (264; *211*).

We may attach to the "instrumentality cluster" a number of further aspects of money to which Simmel draws attention, while referring chiefly (though often implicitly) to a developed money system comprising banknotes and bills of exchange. Under such conditions the instrumental quality of money is heightened by

what Simmel calls its "transportability" (285; *224*) and
its "concealability" (527; *385*). This depends in turn on
the fact that enormous amounts of value can easily be
expressed and conveyed in money terms: a fact that, together with money's "silent" and relatively invisible
character (527; *385*), makes it particularly suitable for
what we could call sub rosa uses. For instance, money
can uniquely assist those who are strangers to a given
society, or occupy in it a marginal position—such as,
typically, the Jews in Western society—in accumulating
economic power (224–28; *221–24*); or it can be used to
bribe officials (526–27; *384–85*). A more positive characterization of money flowing from those same qualities
consists in seeing it as the best possible embodiment of
the notions of moveable, private, personal property
(473; *349*).

A further aspect of money's instrumentality is the
generality of the uses to which it can be put. What Simmel says on this point makes one think of money as a
kind of telephone switchboard which receives messages
of multiple provenance and addresses them to multiple
destinations, or of a large railway station toward which
many lines converge. More abstractly, Simmel quotes
Spinoza's characterization of money as "the compen-
dium of all things" (410; *307*), and conceptualizes it as
"the unconditional terminus a quo to everything, as
well as the unconditional terminus ad quem from everything" (283; *223*).

A second cluster of properties centers on the "impersonality" of money; but this notion in fact covers at
least three distinguishable meanings. In the first place
money is impersonal simply because, as I have already
stressed, it only makes sense *between* at least two per-

sons, and to that extent it transcends each person considered as an isolated entity. This meaning is intensified as the money phenomenon expands and develops, for by the same token money acquires validity not just for a plurality of given, named individuals, but for a broadly defined collectivity, until "it is accepted by everyone from everyone." Each member of the collectivity who receives or spends money implicitly assumes that the whole collectivity takes cognizance of and stands ready to sanction his or her transactions. As Simmel puts it: "Money is a transfer [*Hinweisung*] to the performances of others" (463; *342*).

In a second sense, money is impersonal in that it both presupposes and fosters in those who use it a specific attitude, which we may characterize as detached, cool, or neutral—the mentality appropriate to the selection and handling of a tool, that is of an instrumental facility, a means, rather than to the commitment to an end (267; *212*). On this account, Simmel recounts a piece of advice he had once overheard: never undertake money transactions either with friends or with enemies. "In the first case, the indifferent objectivity of the transaction stands in a never wholly suppressible conflict with the personal nature of the relationship; in the second, that same feature offers much leeway for hostile intentions, which . . . the juridical forms of the money economy can never wholly keep from expressing themselves in willful malice" (290; *227*).

A final meaning of money's impersonality is the following: Its possession affects, shapes, and limits the whole person to a much lesser extent than does the possession of other goods, such as land, or of specialized laboring or professional skills. After all, it is said of money, not of land, or of craft skills, that it and a fool are soon parted. Other forms of possession bring about a much deeper fusion between *Sein* (being) and *Haben* (having) and to that extent, so to speak, stain the person with the history of their acquisition, burden the person with particular demands. Money drastically loosens up that relationship (431; *321*). It does so, paradoxically, because it can be possessed in a fuller, more yielding, more unreserved manner than any other object; thus it does not confront the possessors with any resistance, with any inertia with which they might have to struggle (436–37; *325*). "It is only money that we possess entirely and without reservations, it alone merges entirely with the function we assign to it" (441; *328*).

Money's impersonality makes it a particularly suitable medium for relations whose protagonists seek to minimize their own personal involvement. In the sphere of sexual conduct, for instance, money is prominently associated with prostitution; it closely corresponds with prostitution's nature as "a wholly transitory connection, leaving no trace behind itself." An alternative way of rewarding the prostitute, say the gift of an object, would suit the relationship less because "the gift's content, the choice of it, the uses to which it can be put" tend to bear the imprint of the person giving it much more than the handing over of cash. More generally, "a money transaction implies no commitment," and on that account money can never suitably mediate relationships that require and assume durability and sincerity (512; *376*).

On the other hand, paradoxically, by disengaging the whole person from its possessions, allowing it to distance itself from it, money offers the personality greater opportunity of expressing and cultivating itself.

> Because of its impersonal character and its un-conditioned flexibility, money presents a particularly strong elective affinity with individual achievement and a particular tendency to emphasize it. (461; *341*)

> Money evenly complies with every directive concerning the object of its expenditure, its extent, the speed with which it is expended or retained. In this manner it affords the Ego the most committed and unreserved manner of expressing itself in an object. . . . All that it is and it has, money surrenders fully to the human will, becoming totally absorbed within it. (436–37; *325*)

Having interpreted rather widely the notion of money's impersonality, I see no reason to do more than mention a few other notions one could easily assign to the same cluster, for instance objectivity, impartiality, indifference, or neutrality. My next conceptual cluster (not so distant from the previous one) contains a number of features that I construe as revolving around a central one, the abstract nature of money.

Money is abstract because, to cite again a previous quotation, it "embodies that aspect or function which makes things economic, and which is not all there is to things, but *is* all there is to money itself" (138; *130;* my emphasis). In other terms, money disregards, makes itself indifferent to, many aspects of "things economic" and concentrates its attention on their *economicity* (meaning, as I have repeatedly indicated, their exchangeability). But money can only do this to the extent that it lacks character—an expression Simmel urges us to interpret positively:

> Money has that very positive quality which one designates with the negative concept of lack of character. It is of the essence of the person we term character-less that it does not allow itself to be controlled by the intrinsic, concrete worth of people, things, thoughts, but rather by the amount of power exercised on it by the existing circumstances. The feature of being detached from all specific contents and of consisting in pure quantity imparts to it *and to the people who gravitate toward it* the peculiar coloration of characterlessness. (273; *216;* my emphasis)

Let me mention in passing that the clause I have emphasized in this quotation points up a broad insight of Simmel's. For every institution there is, at any rate in a highly differentiated society, a set of people who are specifically and exclusively identified with and committed to it; and such people often reflect and embody in a particularly intense manner the institution's distinctive traits—whether because their involvement in the institution has so shaped them, or because they already possessed such traits and on that account have specially involved themselves in it.

Turning now to the quotation as a whole, it suggests another feature which I would assign to this cluster—money's exclusive focus on the *quantitative* aspects of reality. Money is quantitative in its very essence, for it expresses numerically the interchangeability of things, it attaches itself to individual things as their price, thus it only exists in specific amounts. "Its quality consists exclusively in its quantity. . . . Quantity constitutes the sole aspect of it which is rationally significant for us; in dealing with money the question is not what and how, but how much" (340; *259*). "In the realm of phenomena, only money loosens itself from any *how* to become wholly determined by its *how much*" (370; *279; my emphasis*).

With this feature of money is associated, of course, its amenability to a distinctive mental process, calculation. Since money can always be added to and subtracted from, and in minute and precise quantities on account of its intrinsic "divisibility" (135; *128*), it becomes the object of calculation par excellence in the sphere of economic life. But in a highly developed economy the resulting mental habits reach beyond that sphere: the "exactness, precision and rigor" required and instilled by economic pursuits tend to apply to the conduct of existence in general (614; *444–45*).

More widely, one may perhaps connect with the quantitative nature of money a property Simmel expressly connects with its characterlessness, one he calls its "knowability": "We know money, as such, more precisely than we can know any other object; for since there is nothing to be known about it there is nothing it can hide from us. On account of its absolute lack of quality, it cannot, unlike the most insignificant other object, keep surprises and disappointments up its sleeve" (316; *244*). On this account, Simmel notes, the progressive expansion of money's role in a society (and most particularly in modern society) is associated with a growing intellectualization of experience, a tendency to orient action reflexively on the basis of cognitive rather than normative expectations (594; *431*).

A final cluster of properties of money centers on what I would call its "potentiality." At one point Simmel uses this expression while seeking to convey a particularly significant, and not wholly obvious, view of money. Avarice, he suggests, points up in a distorted and pathological fashion the property money has of being desirable in spite (or because) of its owner's not intending to put it to any particular use:

> From this standpoint the meaning of money coincides with that of power. Like this, it constitutes a pure being-able-to (*Können*), which stores up an only subjectively intended future in the form of an objectively given present. . . . If somebody asserts that he "can" do something, this designates not only a future event which is being anticipated, but also an already existing state of energy, a set of psychical and physical aptitudes, a definite constellation of available elements. One who "can" play the piano differs, even when he is not playing, from him who cannot, not only in that at a later point he will play it, but already in the present because of an existent, wholly concrete disposition of his nerves and muscles. (313–14; *342*)

To a greater or lesser extent, money confers on those who possess it what we might label the dispositional aspect of possibility. Of course this aspect is most apparent when somebody owns a large amount of money. Simmel notes that the German expression *Vermögen*, "patrimony," often used to designate a largish fortune, means "to be able, to be in a position to." (An expression my mother routinely used to refer to particularly well-heeled people, *gente che può*, literally "people who can," also conveys the quality in question, and again suggests that it is more emphatically present when there is a lot of money around.)

Even in smaller amounts, however, money is associated with choice, and this is an important aspect of what I call its potentiality. Although for any given amount of money all of its uses except one will have to be surrendered when the amount is expended, the divisibility of money makes it possible to commit it in discrete packets, thus encoding and expressing a number of preferences and their respective subjective weightings. Simmel phrases this point as follows, while discussing what I have called the instrumentality of money:

> It is obvious that a tool—other things being equal—will be the more significant and valuable, the greater the number of goals to which it can ultimately be put, the wider the range of possibilities open to its use. . . . Being a means par excellence money fully meets this condition. . . . One might say that the value of a given sum of money exceeds that of any single given object for which it can be exchanged: for it makes choice possible from within an unlimited range of other objects. Naturally it can only be expended for one of them; yet the possibility of choosing is an advantage which adds itself to the value of money. (266; *212*)

More generally, Simmel suggests that money possesses "a metaphysical quality: it extends beyond each particular use of itself and . . . it realizes the possibility of all values as the value of all possibilities" (281; *221*). He makes his point here in somewhat mystifying fashion, but the reader may find an echo of it in a vivid passage from Shakespeare's *Othello*. I am referring to a scene

(1.3) where Iago counsels Roderigo—pointedly desig-
nated among the dramatis personae as "a gulled gentle-
man"—on how to pursue the woman with whom he is
madly infatuated. Desdemona has recently married the
Moor, and Roderigo, despairing, talks about drowning
himself. Iago won't hear of it ("Drown thyself? drown
cats and blind puppies!") and exhorts him to think positive. His main point is that there's no reason for Roderigo to despair of attaining the object of his passion;
but somehow his advice keeps coming back to one
point—money.

> Put money in thy purse; follow thou the wars;
> defeat thy favour with an usurp'd beard. I say,
> put money in thy purse. It cannot be long that
> Desdemona should continue her love to the
> Moor—put money in thy purse—nor he his to her.
> It was a violent commencement in her, and thou
> shalt see an answerable sequestration. Put but
> money in thy purse. These Moors are changeable
> in their wills—fill thy purse with money—the
> food that to him now is as luscious as locusts,
> shall be to him shortly as bitter as coloquintida.
> She must change for youth; when she is sated
> with his body, she will find the error of her
> choice; therefore, put money in thy purse. If thou
> wilt needs damn thyself, do it in a more delicate
> way than drowning. Make all the money thou
> canst. If sanctimony and a frail vow betwixt an
> erring barbarian and a super-subtle Venetian be
> not too hard for my wits and all the tribe of hell,
> thou shalt enjoy her; therefore make money.

One may construe in two ways Iago's refrain about
money. He may be inserting it at random in his speech

as a kind of subliminal command, concealing one of the things he intends—to take advantage of a ninny. (When Roderigo exits, Iago declares to himself, "Thus do I ever make my fool my purse.") But he may also be expressing what I called the potentiality of money, which renders a reference to money plausible and pointed in almost any context. As Simmel puts it, money does by far better than anything else in transcending "the particularity and one-sidedness of all empirical forms." Its abstractness, its characterlessness, allow it to express, select, coordinate, and activate the most diverse and contradictory aspects of "internal and external life" (280; *221*).

I would assign to this cluster two final properties Simmel attributes to money. The first is its dynamic character, which expresses itself in money's tendency to circulate relentlessly from hand to hand, to focus its power on an ever-changing variety of objects and uses: "There is no clearer symbol than money of the absolutely dynamic character of the world. The meaning of money lies in its being expended; when it rests, it ceases to be money as far as its specific value and significance are concerned" (714; *510*). The second property (which could as well be placed in connection with the instrumentality of money) is what could be called the functional character of money; Simmel expresses it by saying that, properly understood, money "does not so much *have* a function as it *is* a function" (201; *169;* my emphasis). Of all possible objects of ownership, "it is only money that merges totally into the function we assign to it" (441; *328*).

As we shall see in a later section, during earlier stages of its development money is appreciated and sought also for its substantive properties; but these later become subordinated and indeed suppressed the more it becomes clear that what you can do with money is all there is to it. On this account, Simmel considers the two parallel and contrasting vices of avarice and greed (the first focused on storing and retaining, the second focused on acquiring, as much money as possible) as phenomena that, whatever their significance, deny rather than affirm money's very nature (308–321; *238–247*).

III.   The Institutional Environment of Money

The heading of this section suggests two distinguishable problems. First, what other major institutional arrangements must be present if money is to exist, to develop, to function effectively? Second, given that money exists and operates, what other institutional arrangements are likely to be associated with it, and particularly with advanced forms of the money economy? Neither problem is discussed expressly or at length in *PdG*, and Simmel gives only scarce and scattered indications concerning the first. They suggest, basically, that the development and the effective operation of money require an atmosphere of generalized trust, going beyond that resting upon the mutual familiarity of the members of a narrow community. Let us see how this can be argued.

As we have seen, money entails a claim to the performances of others (463; *342*); to function properly, it requires everybody's willingness to accept it from everybody. Yet money is merely a symbolic reality; it expresses the mutual exchangeability of things apt to satisfy men's desires while not being itself so apt. Thus that willingness presumes in turn an attitude of trust, a shared awareness of money's virtues and effects and a disposition to act so as to confirm and make use of them. Since each bit of money at bottom constitutes a promise (215; *178*) money can only be routinely accepted if the risk of disappointment is taken to be minimal. Money's ultimate dependency on trust is well conveyed, Simmel notes, by the motto inscribed on a Maltese coin: *non aes sed fides:* what matters is not the bronze (the metallic content of the coin) but the trust. "In the same way that society would fall apart without men's trust in one another—for very few relations actually rest on what one partner knows for a fact about the other, and few would endure at all without a trust at least as strong as, and often stronger than, rational proof and visible evidence—in the same manner without such trust the traffic in money would collapse" (215; *178–79*). The phenomenon of credit, which in its developed form presupposes a money economy, only makes more obvious this dependency of affairs on trust—and a trust, Simmel notes, which is not only "a weak form of inductive knowledge," for it entails a further element of willing, "supratheoretical" commitment, which he does not hesitate to compare with the faith in God (216; *179*).

Simmel's interesting but somewhat generic argument about the diffuse mental and moral atmosphere required for a functioning money economy is complemented by references to two institutional components of that atmosphere. The first, external to the economic realm and to the money phenomenon itself, is constituted by a society's political arrangement. Essentially, if the functioning of money rests on assumptions concerning the conduct of third parties in general, that is, if the money is to be a *public* reality (212–15; *177–78*), then public institutions—above all the state—must back it and sanction it, both by monopolizing the creation of money (249; *200*) and by exercising its jurisdictional powers. In particular:

> For a material as unsubstantial and so easily
> destroyed as paper to function as the carrier of
> the highest monetary value is only possible in a
> cultural setting (*Kulturkreis*) so solidly and tightly
> organized as to eliminate a series of elementary
> dangers, of both an external and a psychological
> nature. (205; *172*)

> It is on the *security* of money that its value
> rests, and central political power progressively
> becomes its guarantor, replacing the immediate
> significance of metal. (224–25; *184*)

The second condition to be satisfied if money is to preserve, as it were, its moral standing in the eyes of people, and thus to function properly, is internal to the monetary realm itself. Money must be *stable*, preserve its value over time. True, in a sense money has no value of its own; or rather, its value consists in money's ability to assess and store the value of *other* objects. But that assessing and storing cannot be reliably performed unless the standard of measurement and the unit of storage remain constant. "[The] significance of money expresses itself empirically as the constancy of value, which clearly depends on money's interchangeability and on its characterlessness. . . . The lengthiness of the sequences of economic activities, which is indispensable to the continuity, coherence, and productivity of the economy, depends on the stability of the value of money. Only this makes possible long-range calculations, complex undertakings, long-term credits" (130; *125*). In the same manner, money exists to circulate, and

thus to mobilize economic values; but to do so effectively it must be a kind of "unmoved mover," constitute
a fixed pivot around which other values may revolve.
Ideally, "money brings about an ever-growing number
of effects, while it remains itself immobile" (204; *171*).

Needless to say, these statements suggest a contrario
how destructive can be the effects of inflation or of other
phenomena that destabilize money, such as deliberate
debasement of the coinage. But Simmel seems to make
them on the assumption that in the modern economy
money does indeed constitute the still center of a series
of increasingly fast-moving and wide-reaching processes of creation and mobilization of value. In fact, it
seems to me, in Simmel's eyes only the stability of
money allows an economic life characterized by its intensely dynamic character to operate within a broader
social environment—fin-de-siècle bourgeois Europe—
which was (or, rather, appeared at the time) distinctively orderly, peaceable, and solid.

Let us now consider some noneconomic aspects of
that environment which, according to Simmel, present
an intrinsic affinity with the central position that
money holds held in it. Since we have already suggested
that the state plays a critical role in making an advanced money economy possible, we may begin with
the political sphere. Concerning this sphere Simmel
gives two main indications. On one hand, the growing
significance of money appears associated with the advance of democratization. For "money is in its intrinsic
nature and on account of its conceptual qualities an absolutely democratic, leveling form, which takes no account of particularistic relationships" (661; *443*). Money's "democratic character," according to Simmel, is

further suggested by the fact that more and more goods, including the products of the "cultural industry" (not Simmel's expression), are marketed on a mass basis, and access to them is open to all comers, as long as they can *monetarize* their interest in them (461–62; *341*).

On the other hand, an important political correlate of a developed money economy is a strongly centralized state, required, as we have seen, to secure an environment in which an attitude of generalized trust can be plausibly entertained by the public (225–26; *185–86*). And that correlate has some significant corollaries. First, the growth of the money economy is associated with the development of public bureaucracies, for—second corollary—it makes possible the regular extraction of economic resources from the larger population by means of taxation (421–22; *315*), and the revenue from this can in turn finance the development of a system of offices (22; *187*). Third, a monetary economy can best function in a legal environment based on state-made, state-backed, positive law, whose interpretation and enforcement rests in principle on a form of juridical discourse which is systematic, concept-based, and rationally controlled (450, 609; *333, 441–42*). Finally, "there is a close correlation between a liberal constitution and the money economy" (691; *495*).

One important reservation must be attached to this last point: "despotism finds in money an incomparably suitable technique, an instrument whereby to tie to itself the farthest reaches of its domination, which in a barter economy always tend to drift apart and to become autonomous" (691; *495*). This disturbing affinity between money and despotism is not as incompatible as it may seem with that mentioned earlier between money and democracy, for Simmel has a Tocquevillean notion of democracy. That is, for him democracy has to do with equality rather than with freedom, and tends therefore to "leveling," for which in turn despotism also has a penchant.

But that reservation does not loom particularly large in Simmel's conception of the political phenomena associated with a money economy. He emphasizes instead the political developments characteristic of Western modernization, and thus those liberal institutions which appeared solidly institutionalized in late-nineteenth-century Europe (though, as we have seen, less so in Germany than in other countries). If the correlation of money with liberalism appeared much more significant to Simmel than its correlation with despotism, this was probably because he saw a developed money economy as associated also with other social tendencies, not exclusively political in nature, whose political implications in turn favored liberalism. He emphasized two such associations, which are closely connected with one another.

In the first place, according to Simmel money was strongly associated with freedom. At the end of chapter 2, I translated a short essay in which Simmel announced the appearance of *PdG* precisely by expounding that association, which he explores at greater length in the book. Money, especially in its developed forms, represents and conveys economic values in such a compendious manner that it allows its owners to loosen themselves from groups which heavily restrict their freedom. They may then constitute or join other groups of a different nature, membership in which commits and controls their energies to a much lesser extent (470;

347). The voluntary, associational, functionally specialized group thus constitutes an institutional development closely associated with the money economy.

Furthermore, even when people remain obligated toward one another or toward groups, money, because of
its impersonal, objective nature, allows them to dis-
charge such obligations while preserving their autonomy to a much greater extent than when they have to offer their personal services or the direct fruits of their
labor (464; *343*). It is on this account that in the agrar-
ian history of Europe the progressive replacement of
the peasants' dues in labor and in nature with money
dues—possibly to be capitalized and paid off once and
for all—had such a liberating influence on the peasants'
existence and their relation to landlords. "The lord of
the manor who can demand of his peasant a given
quantum of beer or poultry or honey, thereby forces the
peasant's activity in a certain direction. As soon as he
merely levies a certain sum of money, the peasant remains free as to whether he will keep bees, cattle, or
whatever else" (378; *286*). Of course this relationship of
money with freedom is most evident when one owns a
great deal of money: it may then impart to one's existence a particularly attractive sense of ease and empowerment, reaching its apex in the ability to be contemp-
tuous of money (280; *220*). In most other cases, Simmel
notes, the freedom imparted by the possession of money
is what he terms "negative freedom": freedom *from*
something rather than freedom *to do* something (549–
50; *400*).

A second phenomenon (closely related to freedom)
with which money is associated is individualization,
the ability for individuals to refer primarily to their
own beliefs, values, and preferences in conducting their

own existence, and indeed to themselves fashion those ideas (469; *346*). Once more, the compressed, compendious way in which money encodes and mobilizes economic values is vital for this association.

> In a nonmonetary economy, the sheer technical difficulty of transferring values over long distances tends to lock them within a relatively narrow economic unit. Its absolute mobility, however, makes of money a link which connects the greatest possible extension of the economic sphere with the greatest autonomization of the personality. The concept which ties together on the one hand money and on the other the growing extension of the economic sphere and differentiation of the individual is that of private property. (473; *349*)

But, as we have already seen, money itself constitutes the best embodiment of the very notion of private property (473; *349*); furthermore, its possession is intrinsically connected with the notion of choice, of elective conduct (267; *212*).

As we have also seen, that possession "most decisively loosens the individual from the unifying bonds which emanate from other objects of possession" (481; *354*). This freedom results from a feature discussed above, the characterlessness of money:

> Money wholly lacks that internal structure on account of which other, specifically characterized things, no matter how much we possess in the juridical sense, deny themselves to our will; money submits itself with equal ease to every form and every purpose the will intends to imprint it with. . . . It yields to every directive concerning the object or the extent of expenditure, the speed of spending it or retaining it. In this

manner it affords the Ego the most decisive and
unreserved manner of expressing itself in an object. (436–37; *325*)

Finally, money frees the individual because it *least* commits his/her *Sein* (being) or *Wesen* (essence) to his/her
Haben (having) or *Besitz* (possession) (410; *307*). On all
these counts the money economy, in its more advanced
states, brings about "an atomization of the individual
person" (463; *342*).

To sum up, then, we may divide the institutional environment of a developed monetary economy into two
parts. The first comprises those conditions that make
possible the development and the sound operation of
the money economy; and these are chiefly a diffuse
sense of trust and those arrangements that can sustain
that sense, that is, a public authority which effectively
backs up and sanctions money with its own distinctive
resources, and the stability of the value of money itself.
The second part comprises institutional arrangements
that present, so to speak, an affinity with a developed
money economy: chiefly, a democratic public order culminating in a centralized state with a liberal constitution, a sophisticated legal system, and arrangements reflecting and protecting the values of freedom and of
individualism.

IV. The Historical Career of Money

Although *PdG*, like other writings of Simmel's, draws
freely on its author's store of historical information, it
contains no sustained discussion of the history (or,
rather, the histories) of the money phenomenon. Simmel directs our attention to various time- and space-

bound circumstances and episodes of that phenomenon, but he does so exclusively to illustrate and exemplify primarily ahistorical arguments. Yet Simmel has a strong sense that money is a historical phenomenon through and through. He clearly shows that the properties of money are more fully and coherently displayed in certain circumstances than in others, that it has been put to varying uses at different times and in different places, and that some aspects of the money phenomenon presuppose and build upon other, more elementary aspects, and to that extent obey a detectable logic of development. He also seems to think that while that logic has, as it were, given notice of itself in several times and places, it has manifested itself more openly and powerfully in the historical experience of medieval and post-medieval Europe than in all other instances. At any rate, he draws chiefly (not exclusively) on that experience in order to identify the main features of that logic; for he seems to feel that how money develops says much of significance about what money is—and vice versa.

The following selective account of what Simmel tells us concerning what I call the historical career of money focuses on two main arguments. I will begin with the one which appears to me to be of greater significance, among other reasons because Simmel sees it as applicable not just to the modern West but also to other historically important manifestations of money, and because he develops it fairly explicitly and systematically (for once!) in two whole sections of *PdG* (chapter 2, sections II and III).

The argument may begin with one of the several conceptual characterizations of money Simmel throws off somewhat casually in his book: "money . . . is nothing but the relation between economic values . . . embodied in a tangible substance" (130; *125*). Thus, on the one hand money expresses, symbolizes, something as abstract as a relation, and that is the *function* constitutive of it and exclusive to it; on the other hand, money presents itself as a object, and to that extent it has a *substantive* aspect that makes it comparable to other objects, and particularly to those whose economic values money itself permits people to assess and transfer.

According to Simmel the first major theme of the historical career of money is the relationship between those two aspects: money as a substance, and money as a function. And within that relationship one may detect a very significant trend, evidenced in repeated developmental sequences at different times and in different places, but most clearly in the modern West: the progressive affirmation of the function over the substance of money. Put otherwise: functional money is ascendant; substantive money is recessive. Let us summarize this argument of Simmel's by sketching an ideal sequence of money forms.

Which substance first counted as money is of course a highly variable matter, as history, archeology and anthropology show. Every time in a given population social development reached the point of suggesting to people that by adopting one category of objects as a general symbol and carrier of value they would facilitate and secure their economic relations, the first category they singled out for such use was generally one they agreed in finding also intrinsically, substantively useful.

The etymology of the term *pecuniary*, which we still use as a synonym for *monetary*, suggests an instance of this. *Pecus* is Latin for sheep (as in pecorino cheese); and in the pastoral phase of the development of the

Latin tribes a sheep was indeed an object of universal economic significance, which on that account would also serve very well as a unit of money. Different populations might of course adopt different categories of objects, but all would share with the Latins' sheep that reassuring quality of immediate utility.

Yet, the more people appreciated in the object in question its ability, qua money, to express, store, and transfer value, the less a sheep or an object of comparable substance would appear appropriate. Most such objects would be rather less handy, accessible, and divisible, less easy to maintain, accumulate, control, count, and transport than one might wish, at any rate if one sought to make money-assisted interactions more frequent, easy, and secure.

The next stage in this ideal evolution of money forms might then be one in which some agreed quantity of a precious metal would serve as a monetary unit. Again, considerable substantive significance still attached to such kind of money. Gold, say, cannot directly satisfy the same basic human needs as a sheep does (you cannot use its fleece as clothing, milk it, cook and eat its flesh, or expect it to reproduce itself), but it has other attractive intrinsic properties: for instance, it is chemically very stable and at the same time malleable and easy to shape; it shines and gladdens the heart, and thus lends itself to the production of a form of money which doubles as ornament (*Schmuckgeld*) and/or which is aesthetically pleasing.

But precious metals also have some unhelpful qualities; their very preciousness generally flows from the fact that they are rare and difficult to refine into pure states suitable, say, for coining. Besides, Simmel notes, the production of and the demand for precious metals are subject to fluctuations which affect their substantive economic value, and which may appear as undesirable perturbations in their functional significance as money. Thus, if money is to sustain and secure a growing volume of transactions, including many which concern small quantities of economic value, this concern with money's function suggests sooner or later that the "tangible substance" involved should include (also) base metals. Again, these may have substantive properties of some significance: some such metals, for instance, can be easily coined into uniform pieces that can be counted or weighed. But one can see that already at this stage what counts in money is more and more its symbolic function, and less and less the material that supplies it also with some substantive properties.

This progression, which in its concrete unfolding presented of course any number of variants, overlaps, reversals, and intermediate steps (for instance, the phenomenon of leather money) had found its provisional culmination, by the time Simmel wrote, in the general recourse to paper money. Often banknotes were meant to stand as mere tokens for a concrete quantity of metallic money for which they could be redeemed, and to that extent referred back to the substantive properties of the metals in question. But in due course paper money lost even this remote connection to a different substantive base and acquired validity purely because it was produced by or on behalf of the state and backed by the state's coercive powers. Furthermore, during its later stages this progression was amplified and complemented by the development of various kinds of instruments of credit, which in turn symbolically represented given quantities of (paper) money (237–38; *192–93*).

The progression in question, which of course since Simmel's time has advanced further through such phenomena as "plastic money," or the encoding of monetary holdings into electronic traces on computer memories, marks for Simmel the ascendance of "functional" over "substantive" money. The "tangible substance" that serves as a support to money, and thus allows it to represent economic values, has all but disappeared, continuing the asymptotic approximation to "the complete elimination of the material basis of money" (234; *191*). Meanwhile, however, money has come to display more and more openly many of the properties Simmel considers intrinsic to it, such as mobility, transportability, potentiality, dynamism—although one may well doubt that it has also preserved the stability that, as we have seen, he considered essential to it.

Thus, the first major trend in the historical career of money is constituted by the ascendancy of function over substance in the makings and workings of money itself. What matters more and more exclusively is money's capacity to represent economic value symbolically. It might be said, in fact, that many economic values are today carried by things—or should we say by events, in the case of the electronic impulses coursing through a computer's processors?—which themselves represent money, and thus bear a more and more remote relation to ultimate economic values.

We might label this trend the progressive sublimation of money; Simmel, provocatively, calls it its "spiritualization" (*Vergeistigung*) (198; *246*), and considers it as inherent in money's nature itself—"money increasingly becomes nothing but money" (609; *441*). And indeed that trend has been in evidence in the vicissitudes of the money phenomenon in many historical situations, even if it has undergone a peculiar acceleration and radicalization in the West. (Though lately it has been suggested that some aspects of that trend previously believed to have originated in the West in the late Middle Ages—such as development of the bill of exchange and of other techniques for extending and securing credit—had in fact developed previously in the context of Islamic commercial practice.)[1]

If the trend toward the spiritualization of money is intrinsically universal because grounded, as Simmel suggests, on the very nature of money, the same thing can only be said with considerable qualification of the second major trend in the historical career of money. This is what may be called the expansion of the money sphere. Over time, that is, money tends to be used in transacting a growing number and variety of economic relations, among other reasons because its transportability allows it to travel over increasing expanses of territory, provided arrangements are put in place to establish its validity, or its convertibility into local currencies (219–221; *180–82*).

This possibly universal tendency has, however, two extremely significant (and closely related) manifestations which according to Simmel were at first exclusive to the modern West. There, in the first place, it is not just a matter of single currencies operating safely over wider and wider territories, or of money being used by a greater and greater number of people to provide for their economic needs. The point is that an increasingly large variety of social relations of the population at large begin to be transacted through money; that, to repeat the Marxian phrasing Simmel himself adopts, "use-values" were almost universally expunged and progressively replaced by "exchange-values." In the "great transformation," as Karl Polanyi has eloquently told us, the reach of the market, and thus of money transactions, originally limited to objects, was for the first time dramatically extended to land and to labor.[2]

The reference to labor brings us to the second distinctive aspect of this second trend, again originally peculiar to the modern West. Elsewhere, money was exclusively the medium of commercial operations, of the buying and selling of objects however produced. The protagonist of money transactions, regularly and gainfully involved in them, was always the merchant or the peddler. In the modern West money begins to be treated as capital, and expressly and aggressively takes charge of the realm of *production* itself. The entrepreneur becomes, to use Marx's imagery, the typical "Money-bags." The "cash-nexus" between employer and employee becomes the chief institutional tool for the activation and coordination of production. Under capitalism, the dominant arrangement for the creation of material wealth becomes "the production of commodities by means of commodities." Thus money becomes, so to speak, not just the horizontal but also the vertical axis of the economy, which in turn, as I indicated, becomes the dominant set of processes over the society at large.

To sum up both the trends Simmel identified in the historical career of money: as it becomes "spiritualized," money becomes also a more and more exclusive and commanding social power. We shall see in chapters 6 and 7 how these two dynamic tendencies affect the nature of modern society.

6

Modern Society (1)

Philosophie des Geldes contains Simmel's most sustained contribution to a task that has always had critical significance for modern social theory: assessing the nature of modern society itself. As I suggested at the beginning of this book, toward the end of the nineteenth century the problem of attaining an understanding of modernity was particularly acute within the German social and cultural sciences, since in Germany modernization had recently advanced at an accelerated pace and in a rather unbalanced fashion, leaving political institutions relatively unmodernized. Furthermore, many German academic intellectuals remained stubbornly attached to what they perceived as the distinctive, uniquely valuable traits of their national culture, under threat from the advance of modernity. Many of them were on that account resolutely (indeed, at times, pugnaciously) critical of other Western national cultures which had earlier, and more spontaneously, accepted or indeed fostered, inspired, and justified the transition to modernity.[1]

Simmel, however, while appreciating and to an extent sharing some considerations and preferences associated with the diffuse German view of modernity as a threat, basically stands aside from that view, or at the very least proposes a highly nuanced version of it. Phrasing it otherwise, modern society as he conceives of it evokes in him great perplexity, but no hostility or aversion. In my two final chapters I argue this point with primary reference to *PdG*, whose "true object," according to Cavalli and Perucchi, is "the historical process of formation of modern society."[2]

PdG, I suggest, conceptualizes and assesses modern society in three principal ways. In the first place, it argues that through the process of modernization some valuable human potentialities, which premodern values and arrangements had left unexpressed, or indeed positively concealed and repressed, come imperiously to the fore. In this sense, I would argue, Simmel views modernity as an "epiphany," that is, as the express manifestation of powers intrinsic to the human species, but previously unrevealed. In the second place, Simmel emphasizes the extent to which modern society at large is shaped and biased by the specific features of an advanced money economy. Finally (and this is the theme of my last chapter) he sees modern society as particularly prone to a complex of processes which together constitute the phenomenon of "alienation."

Before developing the first two notions in this chapter, let me note that, however Simmel may have characterized the adjective *modern* in the expression *modern society*, the noun *society* itself is problematic in his thinking. In their book *Society*, Frisby and Sayer discuss Simmel's understanding of it under the heading of "Society as Absent Concept."[3] They note that in his first book, *Sociale Differentierung*, Simmel criticized two "founding fathers" of sociology as different as Comte and Spencer for assigning "society" a central position in their thinking. By doing so, he felt, those authors had unduly diminished the significance of individuality, reducing the individual to "a point of intersection of social fibers."

As I mentioned in chapter 2, Simmel chose to desubstantialize "society" by placing at the center of his own conception of sociology the "sociation" process [*Vergesellschaftung*]: "Society . . . compared with the *real interaction* of its parts . . . is only secondary, only the result" of that process.[4] *PdG* restates this view in the context of its argument for the general significance of "exchange": "Exchange itself is one of the functions whereby society results from the mere proximity (*Nebeneinander*) of individuals to one another. For society is not an absolute entity which must preexist, and constitute the support and the framework of, its members' single relations. . . . Rather, it is nothing but the comprehensive concept or the general designation of the totality of those reciprocal relations" (208; *174*). This does not mean that Simmel discards the concept of society: in fact he uses it not infrequently and does not always qualify it with an adjective. His *Soziologie*, for example, contains a very significant "excursus" on the theme "How is society possible?" But again what he means there is, basically, How is it possible for individual human beings, constituted as they are, to enter into patterned relations with one another? More generally, Frisby and Sayer suggest, his interest is in those

"microscopic-molecular processes" which "exhibit society in, as it were, *statu nascendi.*"[5]

This interest led Simmel to investigate locales and instances of the sociation process which on the face of it
are little affected by broader and historically more variable social contexts. (He analyzed, for instance, the "so-
ciability" [*Geselligkeit*] characteristic of small gatherings convened merely *for fun* within circles of friends
and associates).[6] Yet such topics coexisted in his thinking with a keen sense for the significance of larger historical contexts. As I said, *PdG* gives evidence of this in
its recurrent concern with the nature of modern society.

Naturally the three themes I distinguish in this chapter and the next (briefly: modernity as epiphany; the
broader impact of the advanced money economy; and
alienation as the human destiny under modernity) overlap, and some aspects of each recur in others. They are
treated separately below, not just to establish a scaffold-
ing for the discussion in the remaining two chapters' argument but also to emphasize the complexity of Simmel's views about modernity. For, it seems to me, the
first argument conveys a largely positive view of modernity, whereas the other two are associated with a growing sense of perplexity. Yet, nowhere does *PdG* express
that "Catonian" rejection of the modern experience so
common among the academic intellectuals of his time,
especially (though by no means exclusively) in Germany.

I. Modernity as Epiphany

As I have already suggested, according to Simmel the
process of modernization has given fuller and more
significant expression to human capacities which previous conditions had left relatively undiscovered and

undeveloped. Modernity speaks more profound truths about the human species than previous cultural legacies and social arrangements had, and indeed it makes possible a better understanding of the making and the makings of earlier conditions than could be attained while the validity of those legacies and those arrangements was still undisputed (58; *421*). (Incidentally, Marx expressed a similar insight in a famous aphorism: "The anatomy of man is the key to the anatomy of the ape.")

If we ask what achievements suggested to Simmel such a positive view of modernity, many of them appear to concern primarily the way reality is typically conceptualized and interpreted in modern society rather than that society's distinctive institutional developments. The advance of modernity, that is, brings what could be called a "cognitive gain." Simmel suggests for instance that "the role of material components in the arts . . . has only very recently been correctly understood" (436; *324*).[7] More generally, Raymond Boudon's thoughtful reconstruction of the contribution of *PdG* to the sociology of knowledge suggests that Simmel saw the typical modern understanding of the nature of knowledge and of its production as superior to earlier understandings.[8]

Yet according to Simmel the boundary between the cognitive and the institutional spheres is a flexible and permeable one; and most modern achievements do establish the cognitive superiority of modern thinking, but only to the extent that they accompany on-going changes in the structures themselves of existence. For instance, according to Simmel, modern conditions acknowledge and affirm two aspects of reality which coexist with and indeed presuppose one another, yet stand to one another in a tension-laden relationship. To wit, the modern mind affirms and enhances at the same time the subjectivity of subjects and the objectivity of objects:

> Essentially, what differentiates the intellectual world of classical antiquity from the modern one is that the latter on the one hand has deepened and sharpened the concept of the ego (conferring on the problem of freedom an extreme significance unknown in antiquity), and on the other has increased the autonomy and strength of the concept of the object, as it expresses itself in the notion that nature obeys unbreakable laws. Antiquity was much closer than later ages to that undifferentiated state in which contents [of knowledge] are represented as such, without apportioning them to subject and object. (30–31; *64*)

But what Simmel has in mind is not just an intellectual development; for in another passage he suggests that, over "the last three hundred years," the modern juxtaposition and contraposition between subjectivity and objectivity has found expression also in concrete structures of everyday existence: "On the one hand, the legality of nature, the material order of things, the objective necessity of events become more and more clear and compelling; on the other, the emphasis upon the independent personality, upon personal freedom, upon autonomy (*Fürsichsein*) becomes sharper and stronger" (403; *302*).

Whatever the balance (or for that matter the causal relationship, if any) between the intellectual and the institutional side of it, I would emphasize that this "parallel development" (403; *302*) constitutes for Simmel the open realization, the *inveramento*, as one says in

Italian, of a basic anthropological datum. For, as we saw in chapter 3, the coexistence and the tension between subjectivity and objectivity are constituent aspects of human nature, evidenced in the ontogenesis of each individual yet differently reflected in the structures of collective existence and in the corresponding presuppositions and strategies of intellectual experience. In my own terms, they find in modernity their joint epiphany. Having insisted on the interaction between what I called the intellectual and the institutional aspects of distinctive modern achievements, I agree with Boudon that *PdG* emphasizes achievements which on the face of it belong primarily to the intellectual sphere, and which concern particularly the possibility of attaining a correct knowledge of reality. The achievements I have in mind can be signaled by two characteristic expressions: on the one hand the principle of the *relativity of knowledge*, on the other the *desubstantialization of reality*. Once more, there is some overlap between the referents of these expressions, but not so much as to make it impossible to consider them separately.

In the vocabulary of Simmel's and his contemporaries, the notion that cognitive constructs, properly understood, had "relative" validity did not have the skeptical implications it gained subsequently.[9] What it asserted was the following: "The contents of thought . . . stand each as the background of the other, so that each receives its meaning and color from the other, and, since they constitute pairs of mutually exclusive opposites, they both call forth one another to generate a possible image of the world, and each of them becomes the ground of proof for the other, via the whole chain of what is knowable" (115; *115*). Thus, whatever is true, is so only with reference to some other truth, *and vice versa.* A telling simile for this relationship is provided by the notion of weight, which is intrinsically relative, in that the weight of any given thing is determined by reference to that of another; thus, of all things taken together it would not make sense to say that they possess any weight at all.

Ordinary cognitive praxis hides this relativity of all truth contents, by treating some of them as the undisputed ground of the validity of others but *not* vice versa—in the same way that, Simmel says, we are more aware of the attraction the moon exercises on the apple than of that the apple exercises on the moon. "As a body may appear to possess weight as a quality of its own, because only one side of the relation manifests itself, in the same manner truth may seem a determination inherent in a given representation in and of itself, because it appears insignificant compared to the totality of those currently assumed as unproblematic. Thus we do not notice the mutual dependency to which all elements owe their truth" (116; *116*, free translation).

The superiority of modern over premodern thinking lies in the extent to which it takes on board "the concept of truth as a relation of representations to one another, not as an absolute quality attaching to any one of them in particular" (103; *108*). For modern thinking the relativity of truth thus understood constitutes "not a qualification which attaches itself to, and weakens, an otherwise independent concept of truth, but the essence itself of truth, the manner in which representations become truths. . . . Truth is valid not in spite of being relative, but on account of being so" (116; *116*).

There is little question that, so understood, the principle of relativity constitutes for Simmel a definite (though perhaps not definitive) advance associated with modernity. The same thing he says emphatically of a methodological strategy he connects with that principle—the preference for "as if" statements. (In 1911 a contemporary of Simmel's, the philosopher Hans Vaihinger, was to expound at length his own understanding of that expression in a controversial book, *The Philosophy of "As If."*) "The assertion that things behave in such and such a way must be replaced . . . by the following: our understanding must proceed *as if* things behaved in such and such a way. This makes it possible to express adequately the way in which our understanding actually relates to the world" (106; *110*).[10]

According to this same passage, the notion of relativity suggests that "constitutive principles, which claim to express once and for all the nature itself of things, should instead be considered as regulative principles, that is perspective points from which to advance knowledge" (106; *110*).

This suggests a relation between the first point, on whose account modernity for Simmel constitutes an *epiphany*, and the second, the modern desubstantialization of reality: it is relativism, Simmel says, that establishes "the (mutual) conditioning of things" as "their essence" (120; *118*). But desubstantialization has also aspects (determinants, concomitants, consequences) of a *noncognitive* nature. It is not just mental contents that implicitly or explicitly refer to one another; rather, under modern conditions it becomes clear that reality itself comprises multiple aspects, none of which stands by itself but all of which presuppose, complement, converge with, contend with, accommodate, subvert, and posit one another. Modernity suggests powerfully (and revealingly) that interaction, mutual effect (*Wechsel-wirkung*) is all there is to reality.

This, as we have already seen, is particularly clear in economic action, which expresses the mutual exchange-ability of objects. (In the term *Wechselwirkung*, mutual effect, widely acknowledged to designate *the* central concept in Simmel's social theory, the first part, *Wechsel*, means "exchange.") Money, in turn, embodies and makes visible that exchangeability. On that same account, it indicates "that things attain their meaning from one another, and that the reciprocity of the rela-tions in which they are suspended confers upon them their being and their determinate configuration [*Sein und Sosein*]"(136; *128–29*). According to Simmel, by the same token money does nothing less than disclose "the formula of being in general." For this further reason, the modern expansion and intensification of the money economy attributes to modernity, so to speak, *epiphanic* significance. It discloses that, in a correct view, reality is not an assemblage of self-standing substances but re-sults from the innumerable effects exercised upon one another by components, each of which derives its own identity from how it relates to all others.

This thoroughly processual view of reality, of course, constitutes the ontological counterpart to the epistemo-logical conception referred to, above, as "relativity." As Donald Levine suggests, for Simmel "the world can be best understood in terms of conflict and contrast be-tween opposing categories";[11] but one might also say that the world results from, consists in, such contrast and conflict. This mutual implication between the ap-propriate conception of knowledge and the appropri-ate conception of reality is particularly clear from the following passage: "Thus, knowing is a freefloating process, whose elements reciprocally determine each other's position in the same way as masses of matter do so by means of weight; for, like weight, truth is a relative concept. If, on this account, our image of the world 'hangs in the air,' this is all right, for so does the world" (100; *106*).

This last statement has, it seems to me, an ironic undertone. It conveys on the one hand Simmel's own resolute conviction of the intrinsic validity of the modern worldview, and on the other his awareness that that view threatened the sense of assurance or indeed complacency many still derived from holding on to premodern views. If this is a correct rendering of the statement's intent, it confirms that according to Simmel humanity owed to modernity a keener consciousness of its own powers (and of the attendant burdens) than it had possessed under previous conditions of society and culture; and that in so (as it were) endorsing modernity Simmel self-consciously distanced himself from positions widely held in his own intellectual environment.

This distancing is also evident if one recalls his statement to the effect that the modern consciousness surpasses that of classical antiquity in its twofold awareness of objectivity and of subjectivity. Throughout the nineteenth century, German intellectuals almost unanimously subscribed to the "myth of Hellas"; for them, Homeric and Attic culture were the highest expressions of the human spirit, nowhere equaled in originality, vigor, and intrinsic validity. The many contemporaries of Simmel's who shared that myth (which, it has been recently pointed out, had some racist undertones)[12] must have found outrageous his suggestion that "the moderns" were superior to "the ancients" on a matter of such significance as the correct understanding of the relationship between objective and subjective aspects of reality.

PdG contains other statements which probably had similar polemical value. It suggests, for instance, that "what we call the objective significance of things lies from a practical standpoint in their possessing validity for a larger circle of subjects" (472; *348*), and that, at bottom, "objectivity = validity for subjects in general" (59; *81*). Simmel also came near to asserting a pragmatist conception of truth (99–100; *106–7*), and associated himself with epistemological positions which allow for "the simultaneous validity of opposing principles" (107; *111*). Finally, although he shared with the majority of turn-of-the-century German philosophers a strong appreciation of Kant's revolutionary emphasis on the significance of a priori components in the knowledge process, Simmel suggested that "much that at one point had been considered a priori, has subsequently been recognized as an empirical and historical construct" (112–23; *114*). Again, these views were probably heretical views within German academia; for their burden, so far as Simmel was concerned, was that the advance of modernity had been associated with a definite, valuable cognitive advance.

II. The Broader Impact
of an Advanced Money Economy

My discussion of the institutional environment of money (chapter 5) has sketched arguments that might have been discussed in this section, since the institutions I previously mentioned tend to develop more visibly and coherently to the extent that money widens its reach and attains sophisticated forms. I am thinking of money's association, for instance, with centralized political power, positive law, or the liberal constitution, for these are all arrangements that in turn characterize modern society as Simmel construes it. Here, however, I will emphasize more abstract phenomena, which to a greater or lesser extent cut across the modern institutional landscape, and which *PdG* connects directly with the growing empire of money. For modern society is characterized not only by the intensification and acceleration of the developmental tendencies of money itself but also by the extent to which money becomes utterly central to it.

One of the several ways in which Simmel phrases this insight is a provoking comparison between money and God. In an important passage (305–6; *236–7*) he applies to money Nicolas de Cusa's characterization of God as *coincidentia oppositorum*, that in which all contrasts are reconciled; suggests that biblical monotheism may have been among the factors predisposing Jews to deal with money in a particularly effective manner; and likens the feeling of peacefulness which money may inspire, because of what I have called its potentiality, to a religious mood. He even argues that these similarities may help account for the recurrent hostility of religious personnel toward money concerns; paradoxically, it is what God and money have in common, rather than what differentiates them from one another, that induces rivalry between them.

Other points mentioned before but which deserve further mention concern the peculiar mental and moral temper associated with modernity. The first aspect of this is the intellectualization of existence, and is connected with the instrumental nature of money (591–92; *429–30*). As we saw in chapter 3, within the context of action evaluations and feelings tend to focus on goals, whereas a cool, cognitive orientation is primarily appropriate to means. The latter orientation, therefore, becomes prevalent in modern society, both directly, because of the central significance acquired by that "tool par excellence," money itself (see chapter 5, above); and indirectly, because under modern conditions money allows the construction of longer and longer means/goals chains, in which more and more of the apparent goals have no ultimate significance but matter purely as means, as way stations to further goals (592; *430*). Furthermore, "the intensification of intellectual, abstracting capacities characterizes our time, in which money more and more becomes a pure symbol, indifferent to its own intrinsic value" (171–72; *152*).

A second, related feature of modernity, clearly associated with the increasing dominance of money, is the premium placed on a quantitative orientation to reality. "Money appears as the exemplar, the expression or the symbol of the modern emphasis on quantitative aspects"–an emphasis which Simmel characterizes as the prevalence of "the interest in how much" over the interest in "what and how," and which according to him "belongs to the very basis of our intellectual constitution" (368–69; *278–79*). That quantitative orientation engenders a disposition to calculate and an emphasis on precision; once more, these are associated with money as well as with another phenomenon in turn related to money: the modern conception of time as a continuous and uniform flow which lends itself to objective, precise reckoning.

The penchant for measuring, weighing, exactly
calculating characteristic of modern times . . .
seems to me causally connected with the money
economy, which makes continuous mathematical
operations necessary in the course of everyday
existence. . . . The mathematical character of
money introduces into the relationship between
aspects of existence the same precision, reliability
in the determination of parity and disparity, lack
of ambiguity in understandings and arrangements, that the general diffusion of pocket
watches imposes upon other external aspects
of our existence. (613, 615; *444, 445*)

Note that, according to Simmel, the quantitative orientation to reality finds expression in very diverse aspects
of the modern institutional environment: for instance, in
the recourse to majorities for settling political conflicts,
or in turning "the greatest happiness for the greatest
number" into an ethical standard (612–13; *443–44*).

A third feature of modernity is the acceleration of the
tempo of existence (706–7; *505–6*). This is clearly connected with money's distinctive ability to mobilize and
transfer values, enhanced in an advanced monetary
economy by the increasingly symbolic character of
money, thanks to which a great number of transactions
can take place very rapidly, for instance on the stock
market (438–39; *325–26*). As indicated in chapter 5, the
growing significance of money imparts a quality of restlessness to modern existence: "The speedy circulation
makes it a habit to give and to receive money, each
specific quantity of which becomes psychologically less
significant and valuable, while money itself acquires
greater and greater importance, for monetary transac-

tions affect the individual more widely and intensely than under less agitated conditions" (247; *199*). And the tension this imparts to modern existence is less likely to be broken by periodic lapses into relative inertia than is the case in societies resting on a natural economy, with their more direct dependence on the rhythms of organic growth (677; *486–87*).

The association with individual freedom we have already attributed to money is also enhanced under modern conditions. A developed money economy allows (or perhaps compels?) individuals to enter into more numerous, wider, more diverse networks of relations with one another. But the relations in question are more and more anonymous, and thus only to a lesser extent commit, nurture, and display the individual's personal qualities (397–98; *299*). Their scope is generally narrow (392–93; *295–96*); their terms are dictated by objective considerations (404; *303*); the resulting associations are "soulless" (468; *346*). Paradoxically, these very features of most of the relations individuals entertain allows them to withhold from them, and to cultivate and express out of their reach preferences and inclinations peculiar to themselves, to maintain a reserve toward their counterparts in those several, uncoordinated, discontinuous, discrete relations (397, 451; *298, 335*).

But there is a dark side to this phenomenon, which Simmel connects expressly, in a passage worth quoting at length, to the increased recourse to money, which is related in turn to ongoing modernization:

> The relationships of modern man to his milieu generally develop in such a way as to distance him from those closest to him in order to bring him close to those more distant. . . . In this gen-

eral picture we find that distance increases within properly intimate relations, while it diminishes within more external ones. . . . The extent and intensity of the role money plays in this twofold process manifests itself at first as the *overcoming* of distance. . . . But money seems to me more significant as the medium of the opposite tendency. . . . Money transactions create barriers between those involved, since only one of them receives what he *actually* wants, what activates his specific sensations, while the other at first only receives money, and must seek what he wants from a third party. The fact that each enters the transaction with a wholly different *kind* of interest imparts a new element of estrangement to the antagonism already resulting from their contrasting interests. . . . In this manner, as I said, there emerges an inner barrier between people, one however that is indispensable for the modern form of existence. (664–65; *476–77*)

Those discussed so far are aspects of modernity connected with the formal properties of money, and thus those intensified by the growing scope and sophistication of an advanced money system. We may now return to a point made at the beginning of this section, concerning the central position money occupies in modern society. If we consider in this light the intrinsic nature of money, rather than its formal properties, we realize that such position expresses and enforces in turn the centrality of economic values, the dominance within modern society of the processes pertaining to the production and distribution of wealth.

As we shall see in a moment, Simmel is emphatically aware of this aspect of modernity; but *PdG* chiefly investigates its significance for the culture, the mentality, the life-style of modern society, rather than showing how it shapes (and results from) the distinctive struc-tural arrangements of modern society, its stratification system, the nature of its major component groups, and the pattern of the relations obtaining between them. (Characteristically, the final chapter of the book bears the title "The Style of Existence," not "The Styles"; and throughout *PdG* Simmel reveals both his aware-ness of the class phenomenon and his relative lack of interest in it.)

Within these limitations, *PdG* argues most eloquently and in a very sophisticated fashion the pervasiveness and depth of the effects the money phenomenon has upon modern society. I have already mentioned some of those effects, and I will leave aside others—particularly those of a sociopsychological nature—except when they are relevant to the problem of alienation. In the balance of this chapter, I will just consider some of the general statements directly addressing the relationship between money and modern society.

> At present . . . the whole shape of existence, the relations of men to one another, the objective culture receive their color from the interest in money. (304–5; *236*)

> Money becomes the central and absolute value. (369; *279*)

> The whole heartlessness of money mirrors itself in the culture of society, which it determines. (468; *344*)

A correlate of this overpowering presence of money is "the materialism of modern times, which even in its theoretical significance must share a common root with their money economy" (360; *273*). Under modern law, for instance, it is difficult to seek remedy and compensation for individual interests, no matter how unjustly damaged, unless those interests are of a patrimonial nature, and a money equivalent can be given for them; most of the values that cannot be evaluated in those terms are practically disregarded by the apparatus of justice. This is, as it were, the downside of the "extraordinary simplification and uniformity" achieved by the modern legal system (503; *369*).

A concomitant of such materialism is of course an accentuated secular orientation, the individuals' growing inability or unwillingness to keep themselves attuned to transcendental beliefs and values. This phenomenon, Simmel notes, had already occurred during the decadence of Greece and Rome (305; *236*); but it has particularly damaging effects in (post-)Christian societies. For, with Christianity, "for the first time in the history of the West a real ultimate purpose of life was offered to the masses, an absolute value of existence, beyond all that was petty, fragmentary, contradictory in the empirical world: the salvation of the soul and the kingdom of God. . . . [In this way] Christianity allowed the need for an absolute, ultimate purpose to sink such deep roots, that even those souls who now reject it inherit from it a longing for a definitive purpose of existence as a whole" (491; *361*). Therefore, *modern* secularization—in which, I repeat, the advance of the money economy plays a critical role—leaves man particularly deprived: he has lost any sense of ultimate purpose, but still longs for one.

A final aspect of modern society which one may relate to the central position of money within it is what Simmel labels the objectivity of the modern life style. Money, operating as the universal link between all aspects of reality, brings everywhere its distinctive features of impersonality, abstractness, calculability, and so on. Individuals are thus made to feel that they inhabit an immense and diverse but unified, self-enclosed realm of objects, all parts of which relate to one another and to the whole as if mechanically, leaving no place for emotion or for a sense of purpose or hierarchy.

> Insofar as money itself is the omnipresent means to all goals, all elements of existence are geared together into a colossal teleological complex in which none of them is first and none is last. And since money measures all things with pitiless objectivity, and their resulting value determines their connections, there emerges a web of material and personal aspects of life which approximates the unbroken cohesion and the strict causality imparted to the cosmos by the laws of nature. Everything, here, is held together by money value in the same way that nature is held together by all-activating energy. Both energy and money value vest themselves in a thousand different forms, yet the uniformity of their nature and the reversibility of all their transformations connect anything with anything and make of anything the condition of anything. (593–94; *431*)

A world centered on money is thus a unified world, but one which gains its coherence only from objective relations, not from giving expression to a meaningful design on which individuals may fasten their commitments and their hopes. In Wittgenstein's inimitable statement, instead, "The world is all that is the case."

In so analyzing the hold upon modern society of an advanced money economy, Simmel began to introduce markedly negative motifs into his appraisal of modernity. It is difficult not to detect a strong critical charge in a phrase like the following: "If modern man is free— free because he can sell everything and free because he can buy everything . . ." (555; *404*). Those motifs are even more clearly in evidence in *PdG*'s argument about alienation, to be reviewed in the next chapter.

7

Modern Society (2)

The last (and, in my judgment, best) chapter of *Philosophie des Geldes* has as its main theme the phenomenon of alienation, which Simmel considers central to the modern condition. But that theme recurs in other writings of his, and most particularly in "The Concept and the Tragedy of Culture," which for that reason I shall repeatedly draw on in this chapter.[1] In fact, such is the significance of alienation in Simmel's contribution to social theory that it would justify applying to him the expression "the Marx of the bourgeoisie," which others have used for Max Weber or Karl Mannheim. (A tenable case could be made, incidentally, to the effect that "the Marx of the bourgeoisie" is Marx himself.) At any rate, both the prominence of the alienation theme in *PdG* and its strong bearing on our concern in these last two chapters—the nature of modern society—suggest that we consider briefly a few other authors who have also entertained that theme (whether designating it as alienation, or estrangement, or reification).[2]

I

Although one may argue that the theme (if not the notion) of alienation is already present in Rousseau,[3] it definitely enters the history of modern social theory with Hegel. Marx, however, constitutes a more proximate source of its enduring significance, both because his treatment of the theme is less exclusively philosophical than Hegel's, and because it has had a great deal of broader intellectual resonance. (Some people might claim, too great a deal.) In Marx's thinking itself, the notion of alienation is primarily a conceptual tool for a critique of the condition of wage laborers under capitalism. But even in this apparently narrow understanding of it, that notion is anything but univocal. Its complexities may be suggested by the titles of two Marxological works of some significance, where the term *alienation* is juxtaposed with two vastly different other expressions. The title of a book by Pierre Naville, *De l'aliénation à la jouissance*, implies that for Marx alienation was essentially a subjective condition of the worker, which the socialist revolution would negate and transcend by making workers experience "enjoyment."[4] The title of a book by Andrew Gamble and Paul Walton, *From Alienation to Surplus Value*, implies instead that in the writings of the young Marx the notion of alienation foreshadowed philosophically an objective condition—the exploitation of the worker by the capitalist—which his later writings would analyze in depth within a scientific framework.[5]

If this already indicates, as I have suggested, the complexities of the word in question in Marx's own thinking, they become even more evident if one considers the scope attributed to it by other significant Marxological writings. A significant book by Yves Calvez, for instance, reconstructs all of "La pensée de Karl Marx" as an exploration of multiple forms of alienation—religious, philosophical, political, economic—which do not only affect workers, but characterize the entire condition of humanity before the advent of socialism.[6]

One may object that these interpretations render excessively broad the Marxian notion of alienation. Yet that breadth is justified by various texts of Marx's own. The most impressive and inspiring of these, I think, is a brief note Marx jotted for himself in 1846, while working with Engels on the manuscript of *The German Ideology*: "The individuals always start out from themselves, take themselves as points of departure. Their relations are relations of their real life process. How does it happen, then, that their relations acquire autonomy over against the individuals themselves? that the powers of their existence overpower them?"[7] This—it seems to me—exceedingly pithy and pathos-laden passage suggests a very broad understanding indeed of the phenomenon of alienation. In the light of it Marx can claim the status of one of the protagonists of (among other things) modern philosophical anthropology, in which such a broad understanding is often entertained—in a variety of formulations and elaborations.

Before undertaking a brief analysis of that understanding, I will note that the passage I just quoted from Marx has a distinct undertone of puzzlement, which it shares with other more famous texts (for instance, Rousseau's "Man is born free, yet he is everywhere in chains"). Perhaps the puzzlement in question arises from the characteristic modern contrast between on the

one hand the self-confident pride in the human creative powers uncovered by Western post-Renaissance
thought, the exalting sense of man's ability to make and
unmake social reality and himself, and on the other the
awareness of the inadequacies, fallacies, and miseries of
existent conditions. If man is such a wondrous thing,
why oh why does he not clean up his act?

Of all the experiences which may inspire such puzzlement, the most puzzling (and the one best characterized
in that early Marx text, as well as in Simmel's own contribution to the alienation theme) is the persistent and
frustrating sensation that the products themselves of
human activity, the objects in which are embodied the
powers of the species, systematically escape man's control and frustrate his purposes. On this understanding,
the core of the alienation phenomenon is the *autono-
mization* of human artifacts, their progressive diver-
gence from the intentions and projects presiding over
their production.

The theorization of this experience (with or without
the use of *alienation* and equivalent expressions) reaches
beyond Marx, Simmel, and the philosophical anthropology tradition to much of social theory at large. Only
consider, for instance, Weber's rendering of the historical transformation of capitalism. Having arisen as
(among other things) the religiously inspired moral
project of individuals seeking to prove their good standing in the eye of God, capitalism turned into a self-
standing "cosmos," an "iron cage." Or consider again
Weber's sharply phrased account of the associated shift
in the specific ethical content of entrepreneurship and
associated occupational duties: "The Puritan wanted to
be the man of his calling [*Berufsmensch*]; we *have to* be."

This broad view of the alienation phenomenon is generally conveyed by one or more of a few topoi, of striking expressions that recur insistently in the corpus of classical social theory and which suggest various (but sometimes overlapping) aspects of that phenomenon. I shall list three such topoi. The first is to the effect that in human affairs there often occurs an inversion of cause/effect relationships, as in the following quote from *Das Kapital*: "For example, here is a man who is king only because other people behave as his subjects. Yet they, for their part, believe themselves to be his subjects because he is king."[8] A second topos points up the inversion of subject/object relations. *Das Kapital*, again, contains innumerable statements to the effect that capital obeys its own immanent logic of "valorization," with respect to which all individuals involved, including the capitalists themselves, are simply instruments. Thus things (for instance, the stock of productive resources vested in an enterprise) behave as subjects, that is as entities with interests and powers of their own; and subjects behave as things, as entities at the service of alien interests and powers. As we shall see, this aspect of alienation is very significant in *PdG*. Let one quote suffice here: "The cultural objects grow more and more into a complex which hangs together, and which at fewer and fewer points comes into contact with the subject's soul, with its will and emotion. And the complex the objects constitute is more and more carried forward by their self-activating motions. . . . Material as well as mental objects, today, move about of their own initiative, without individuals supporting them or carrying them around" (638–39; *460*).

A third topos—the inversion between means and goals—is so significant in Simmel's thinking that we shall consider it at some length below. Among other social theorists, it is probably best articulated by a contemporary of Simmel's, Robert Michels. Without explicitly relating this argument to a concept of alienation, Michels eloquently argued in his most famous work, *Political Parties*,[9] that socialist parties and unions, originally formed as instruments of working-class interests, tend subsequently to disregard such interests, and to make their own survival and aggrandizement their sole effective concern. Later sociologists have derived from this argument the view that organizations are prone to a process of "goal displacement."

The attentive reader will have noted that these three topoi have one thing in common: they all construe different processes of *inversion*. And indeed "inversion" is, in my view, the most powerful metaphor in much theorizing about alienation. Time and again, such theorizing puts forward the imagery of a forceful turning of the tables, of a paradoxical twist imparted to reality, of things being turned on their heads, or having an unexpected, redoubtable direction imparted to them (as in the German expression *Umschlagen*).

What, one may ask, is being turned upside down, twisted around, subverted? At bottom, if I understand Simmel correctly, what alienation *happens to* (so to speak), is the human authorship of social reality. As suggested above, it is objects embodying and expressing the powers of the human subject that invert their original relationship to that subject, by escaping its reach, denying themselves to its purposes, frustrating them. If we thus understand it (and again I am trying to convey

Simmel's view of it) the whole alienation phenomenon connects both directly and paradoxically with the notion of objective spirit. It represents the vexing outcome of human creative powers whose expressions, again, turn away from and against their originators, to the extent that they no longer experience those powers as belonging to them nor benefit from their exercise.

If this is a correct rendering of Simmel's view of alienation (and that of others) we may distance ourselves for a moment from it and ask ourselves how one might discount the significance of the alienation phenomenon and the attendant pathos. It seems to me that in modern social theory there is a fundamental, recurrent argument (in multiple variants) for, as it were, "cooling" the talk about alienation in its multiple forms. To begin with, the recurrent imagery of human products which perversely deny or oppose their producers' intents may betray a basic misapprehension. The wondrous powers that alienation supposedly frustrates are not those of specific individuals but those of the species; and the moaning and ranting about alienation ignores the unavoidable dependency of the former on the latter. The individuals who complain about the poor correspondence between their designs and their products' logic of motion are simply mistaken: normally, those are not in fact *their* products anyway. Humans, as cultural animals, normally avail themselves of their predecessors' activities; but if those results are to endure over the generations perforce each successive generation must accept what is handed over to them as a datum, with an inertia and a logic of its own.[10]

More widely, one may argue that, by curbing the individuals' awareness of their power to make and unmake social reality, alienation does them a great service. For if individuals were continually aware of that power and intent upon asserting it, endless, wasteful tinkering with whatever arrangements exist would result. Furthermore, their different perspectives and interests would induce individuals and groups to bicker invidiously and struggle destructively over what shape to impart to reality. To avoid such conflict, it is salutary that people should view as *sacred*, as embodying a higher, unchallengeable, uniquely valid design, even things that are of their own making and to that extent intrinsically open to further intervention. In fact, if people did not learn to take for granted some things— indeed, the overwhelming majority of things—they would never find the time and the energy to innovate on them at the margin, which is the only way they can further enrich and improve upon the legacy of the past. In sum: cultural legacies cannot deliver their benefits to living human beings unless humans accept such legacies (also?) as legitimate burdens.

This way of arguing that, as it were, alienation is good for you, has sometimes a corollary, to the effect that those who protest against it and try to resist or suppress it are intellectually feeble and morally puerile and should be ashamed of themselves. The noblest formulation of this argument is that whereby Socrates, in Plato's dialogue *Crito*, justifies his decision not to escape from the prison where he is detained and to drink the hemlock, complying with the (however unjust) sentence of death pronounced upon him by an Athenian court. He tells his disciples, who urge him to make use of the arrangements they have made for him to escape, that overnight he has had a vision of the Laws of Athens, reproaching him for even contemplating an escape. If Socrates fled the death now imposed on him, the Laws say to him, that would mean that, after availing himself throughout his life of the advantages the Laws have conferred on him as a citizen of Athens, Socrates would have disowned his resultant obligations toward them, and in order to avoid his own destruction destroyed them by setting their decree to naught—and what an immature and irresponsible way of acting that would be! The reader may find some traces of this critique of the concept itself of alienation in the argument by Simmel reviewed below. But essentially Simmel endorses that concept, and presents a vigorous and original version of it.

II

As I have already indicated, Simmel's conception of alienation is rooted in the notion of objective spirit. Alienation represents a fateful vicissitude in the relationship between subjects and objects; it expresses on the one hand their mutual dependency and their similarity of nature (represented, as I have suggested, by the noun *spirit* as against the adjectives *subjective/objective*), and the other hand their tendency to diverge (their *Diskrepanz*, Simmel calls it), their repeated, frustrating failure to acknowledge one another.

To understand why this occurs, we must reconsider one property of the embodiments of the objective spirit discussed in chapter 4. Besides being publicly accessible, external realities which "bind time," objects are of necessity externally bounded, internally bonded, structured entities. That is, they only exist in certain configurations and have a given form and distinctive qualities. Although the objects we are talking about are the product of past action, those qualities of theirs are of consequence for future action: they open up certain possibilities and foreclose others. To repeat a previous quotation: "Only to the extent that a given object is something for itself, can it be something for us" (435–36; *324–25*).

Although this point is most obvious in the case of material objects, Simmel elaborates it also with reference to objects of other kinds; for instance, to interaction patterns, such as those dependent on the number of interaction partners (see chapter 4), or to language. Although language is a human product, and the medium of man's most distinctive achievements, Simmel says, "sometimes we experience language as an estranged force of nature which bends and frustrates not just our expressions, but even our most intimate thought processes."[11] For there is no such thing as *language;* only languages exist, each as a peculiar set of structures which lends itself to certain communicative uses and by the same token precludes others.

The point of this for the argument about alienation is already indicated in the very term *object*, where the root *ob* indicates, in Latin, opposition, resistance; and this holds also for the equivalent German term *Gegenstand*, where *gegen* means "against." And the point is that objects can only assist action to the extent that they resist it: "Only insofar as [an object] sets boundaries to our freedom does it make room for it" (436; *325*).

How this bears on alienation is best discussed by Simmel in "The Concept and the Tragedy of Culture." In that essay *culture* has a specific meaning, best approximated by the English noun *cultivation*, as the condition of being or the process of becoming conversant with products of high intellectual or aesthetic significance, or by the adjective *cultured* as characterizing a person who is familiar with such products for other reasons than as an aspect of his or her professional activity.

Simmel conceptualizes being cultured, possessing culture, in this sense, as the result of a sustained series of successful encounters between a given person's "subjective spirit" and (a number of aspects of) the "objective spirit" surrounding that person. A successful encounter is one whereby the person is challenged (not just entertained), enhanced (not just instructed), made more aware and sophisticated (not just more knowledgeable) by what he/she learns and experiences in his/her intercourse with the products of others' intellectual and aesthetic activity. In other words, a successful encounter, an accomplished episode of "cultivation," is one in which those products act on the person initiating the encounter, so that he/she returns subjectively enriched to him/herself from the encounter. Ideally, this may empower the person to produce further objects; but the essential point is the ability to absorb the existent object, metabolize it as it were, assimilate it to his/her own subjectivity.

What makes this possible is, in my own terms, the commonality of noun between subjective and objective spirit—the fact, as Simmel says, that "both parties are spirit"; thus the subject can both recognize itself in the object and express its own powers within the realm of objects, enriching the latter and not just itself. But if that is possible it is not always easy; in fact, it tends to be difficult, and particularly so under modern

conditions. The root of the difficulty lies in the very ob-
jectness of cultural objects, in the resistance they pose,
which must be mastered if the subject is to have its way
with it; for, alternatively, the object itself will have its
own way with the subject, distracting him/her from his/
her own cultivation. "The Concept and the Tragedy of
Culture" characterizes this second outcome as follows:
"The spirit brings about self-standing objects, over
whose path must take place the development of the subject from itself to itself. But by the same token is initi-
ated the autonomous development of those very objects.
This development continuously consumes the energies
of subjects, drags them along *without* leading them to
fulfill themselves. Thus the subject's development can
no longer follow the same road as that of the objects,
and if it follows that road it runs itself into a cul-de-sac
or a vacuum."[12] The "tragedy of culture" lies in the fact
that, in Simmel's judgment, this development is more
likely than the alternative one, which sees the subject
come out of its encounter with cultural objects enriched, empowered, "cultivated." Why should the first
outcome be more likely, and particularly so under modern conditions?

III

The basic reason for unfulfilled development is straight-
forward and can best be given in quantitative terms. In
modern society, the accumulation of knowledge, of
skills, of technical resources, of the machinery of civilization has reached a point where it yields as if automat-
ically an overwhelming number and variety of products. While most individuals have some access to a

varying but relatively high proportion of those products, none have a chance of *mastering* more than a ridic-
ulously insignificant proportion. Rather, they mostly
"traffic" with objects—material and cultural—and become dependent on them, without understanding them
and often without truly appreciating them.

A subheading from chapter 7 in *PdG* characterizes in
lapidary fashion the resulting, fatal *Diskrepanz:* "Increase in the culture of things, lag in the culture of individuals." Let us try to organize into a coherent discourse the many disparate components of the argument
Simmel conducts to this effect in *Philosophie des Geldes*
(and in other writings, among these one of his most famous essays, "The Metropolis and Mental Life" of
1903). Under modern conditions, the alienation phenomenon flows, in the first place, from the processes
that produce material and cultural objects. Two overlapping aspects of those processes make it very difficult
for their protagonists to recognize themselves in their
products, to sense that their own powers are embodied
in them.

The first aspect is the advanced division of labor
characteristic of modern production (628–31; 435–56).
This makes the production process very complex and
locks its individual participants into narrowly circumscribed, highly specialized working roles. Mostly, their
operations are imperiously prescribed, directly by the
machines to which they attend and indirectly by the
managerial requirements of a complex productive unit
which they cannot survey or understand. "A working
performance strongly and self-consciously based on the
division of labor intrinsically tends toward the category
of objectivity. The worker himself is ever more likely to

consider and carry out his performance in a purely objective and anonymous fashion, and thus it no longer reaches the roots of his life as a whole" (630; *455*).

The second aspect is the capitalistic structure of modern industry. Simmel argues its effects in ways which may remind readers of Marx's discussion of "alienated labor" in a text well known today but unknown to Simmel himself and his contemporaries.[13] Workers, Simmel says, are typically "separated" from the means of production; from the work experience itself, which is carried out under the control of employers and their agents; and from the products of labor, for these are commodities, and as such possess "laws of motion of their own, a character foreign to that of the producing subject himself" (631–33; *455–57*).

Furthermore, the "growing estrangement between the subject and its products" (637; *459*), induced by the division of labor and by capitalism in what Marx would call "the sphere of production," finds a parallel in that of consumption. Normally, under modern conditions, individuals consume and otherwise make use of objects which are produced not for them but for the market, and which reach them through complex distribution arrangements: "So many intermediate passages stand between the producer and the consumer that they wholly lose sight of one another" (633; *457*). Besides, the offerings of the market are so numerous, diverse, and changeable that the consumer rarely has a chance of acquiring a thorough, self-confident familiarity with what he/she owns and uses. As is particularly clear in the case of fashion, products incessantly and invitingly present themselves to the individual as if they were part of "a self-activating movement, an objective force which evolves through powers of its own" (641; *461*).

As a result, even in their capacity as consumers individuals feel overwhelmed by the objects which surround them, and which they cannot easily assimilate; and this feeling is enhanced under modern conditions, as Simmel suggests by listing

> the multitude of styles with which we are confronted in objects we see everyday, from houses to the design of books, from sculptures to gardens and furnishings, in which Renaissance and Japanese styles, Baroque and Empire, the Pre-Raphaelite style and that of matter-of-fact functionalism stand next to one another. . . . This multiplicity is confusing. . . . Each style is like a distinct language, which employs determinate sounds, morphology, syntax to express life; and only as long as we know just one style which we share with our milieu does it not confront us as an independent power with an existence of its own. . . . Only a plurality of styles on offer detaches each of them from its specific content, confronting our freedom to choose one or the other of them with its own autonomy and the significance it independently possesses. (641–42; *462–63*)

"The Concept and the Tragedy of Culture" suggests that the diversity and changeability of the potential objects of possession and consumption may induce the individual who aspires to cultivation to a self-defeating strategy aimed at facile acquaintance, superficial connoisseurship, motivated by an ambition to keep oneself up to date with whatever is new, say, in the arts. Unavoidably, such a strategy displaces or detracts from *il lungo studio e il grande amore,* the protracted effort and the loving commitment which, according to Dante's invocation to Virgil at the beginning of *The Divine*

Comedy, are necessary for the individual to achieve cultivation. On the other hand, those who thoroughly immerse themselves in a field of artistic or literary scholarship, Simmel warns, may also lose thereby their subjective ability to appreciate in a fresh manner the aesthetic value of the works they deal with; their own effort at cultivation may fail under the weight of their hard-won technical expertise.

Another way of considering the enormous accumulation of objects which characterizes modern society was suggested in chapter 6. Most of those objects only play an intermediary role in very lengthy means/goal chains, and have no intrinsic significance of their own. This role has two "alienative" consequences. In the first place, as we have seen, trafficking with such objects (as producers, consumers, whatever) only activates and fosters—at best—the intellectual powers of the people involved. Such powers fasten on those objects' instrumental import and disregard their insignificance from the standpoint of values and emotions. "This preponderance of means over goals finds its culmination and its most comprehensive expression in the fact that the periphery of life, matters outside of life's spiritual significance, have come to dominate over its center and over ourselves" (672; *482*).

What this engenders, or reinforces, is the view of the world as "all that is the case," as a complex of units and events held together only by causal processes, in which it is difficult to find purpose and meaning. In order to exist in a world so conceived, individuals must, as it were, bracket their own subjectivity and concentrate on tinkering with objects, operating them as effectively as possible. This engages them in an effort at mastery over means: but the set of means they can realistically seek to master is generally very small. Besides, as Simmel notes in a different context, often a serious effort to master something takes the form of subordinating oneself to what one wants to master (317; *245*). This subordination is reflected in the central position technology occupies in modern society: "The control over nature which technology offers us is paid for by our enslavement to it" (672; *482*).

Insofar as this occurs, there opens up a second "road to alienation," suggested by one of the topoi mentioned above: the tendency for means to become goals in themselves. And here, again, money comes in, and nowhere as triumphantly as in its modern, highly developed forms. Money is, as we have seen, intrinsically and exclusively instrumental; it owes all of its significance to its ability to give access to things other than itself, which alone can directly satisfy human needs. But this ability money possesses to such an extent, it can open so many doors so easily and effectively, that, paradoxically, it becomes the pinnacle and the center of most people's aspirations, ambitions, and wants, and it tends to acquire a powerful hold over their passions. "Money is the absolute means that on that very account acquires the psychological significance of an absolute goal" (307; *238*).

Today more than ever, the multiplicity and complexity of means/goals chains, Simmel writes, "is brought about by money, for money constitutes an interest which connects otherwise unrelated chains, to such effect that any one of these can serve as the premise of another wholly unrelated to it in substantial terms. . . . What counts is the fact . . . that everywhere money is conceived as a goal, and thus degrades to means an extraordinary number of things which properly constitute goals" (593; *431*). The sovereignty and centrality of money interests in modern society, then, amounts to a massive "inversion" and thus (as we have seen) to a massive phenomenon of alienation, connected with other modern manifestations. Advanced forms of the division of labor, for instance, are only possible in a money economy: "Only the exclusively monetary relation [between the employer and the worker] has that utterly matter-of-fact and automatic character which is indispensable to the construction of very differentiated and complex organizations" (65; *468*). "Only money allows cultural objects to develop the degree of autonomy, the compelling form, which makes them resemble the way nature holds together" (651–52; *469*).

IV

The position held by Karl Marx in my brief discussion of the concept of alienation at the beginning of this chapter raises the question of the relationship between Marx's version of that concept and Simmel's own. I may begin to address that question by remarking that the relationship is, for one thing, a genealogical one, in the sense that Simmel's thinking about alienation (as well as about other matters not discussed expressly in this book) was influenced by Marx's—although, as I have already remarked, some close parallels obtain between Simmel's arguments in *PdG* and some arguments of Marx's of which Simmel did not know.[14] In particular, in "The Concept and the Tragedy of Culture" Simmel expressly gives Marx's "fetishism of commodities" as an example of the phenomena he is himself concerned with.

Furthermore, I would say that alienation holds comparable significance for Simmel and Marx in their views about modern society, at any rate as far as Marx's early writings are concerned. Finally, there are some impressive similarities of form and substance between the respective arguments. To give just an example, if readers return for a moment to the passage I quoted from *The German Ideology* in section I of this chapter—a passage unknown to Simmel—they will see remarkable similarities between that passage and one from chapter 7 of *PdG*, in which Simmel comments on the growing discrepancy between "the culture of things" and that of individuals: "How can one explain this phenomenon? If, as we saw, the culture of things is but a culture of men, so that we give shape to ourselves only by giving shape to things, what is one to make of the fact that the development, elaboration and intellectualization of things advances as if according to powers and norms of its own, and without the minds of individuals becoming correspondingly developed?" (622; *449*).

Having thus briefly compared Simmel's views on alienation with Marx's, I will as briefly contrast them. I see a few significant (and overlapping) differences. In the first place, although (as I have emphasized) for Simmel modernity intensifies the experience of alienation and widens its reach, he considers alienation a phenomenon inherent in the human condition; philosophically, he construes it as a variable but unavoidable aspect of the relationship between subjective and objective spirit. (In his later writings, he made this point by theorizing both the indispensability of "forms" to "life"— "We *are* life in an immediate sense . . . but we *possess* life only in this or that form"—and the irreducible contrast between the two.)[15] In sum, alienation is for

Simmel an anthropological datum, the fate of the species. As to Marx, one may argue whether he considered alienation a phenomenon only of capitalist society or attributed forms of it to earlier societies; but there is little doubt that for him the advent of socialism would eliminate the phenomenon, proving that it arose not from the nature of man but from specific historical conditions which the revolution would suppress.

In the second place, Marx considered alienation—or at any rate its most significant historical manifestation, capitalist alienation—as conceptually a yes-or-no phenomenon, for it rests on expropriation, on direct producers being forcibly deprived of control over their products. For Simmel alienation is a less clear-cut matter: any given manifestation of it constitutes a particular vicissitude of the relationship an individual has to a set of objects—and conceptually that vicissitude may be probable (especially so under modern conditions) but is not necessary, nor is it always irreversible. What happens, say, when someone visits a museum, is always a contingent matter: the visitor may or may not become more "cultivated," depending on how he or she handles the experience.

A closely related difference is the following. For Marx alienation is an aspect of the relationship between individuals, or (perhaps more correctly) between classes; it is, crudely put, something the exploiters inflict upon the exploited. For Simmel, as I have just indicated, it is an incident in the relationship between individuals and objects, an incident which in turn reflects an unavoidable tension between subjective and objective spirit (or, in the language of the later Simmel, between life and forms). Even though Simmel emphasizes the alienation experienced by wage workers, he describes the world of production and the attendant alienation forms in terms that are class-blind. "Production, with its technology and its results, appears as a cosmos with established, logical as it were, features and trends of its own, which stands to the individual in the same way as fate stands to the instability and irregularity of the will" (651; 469).

Although Simmel implicitly agrees with Marx in seeing economic alienation as a phenomenon utterly central to modern society, each construes somewhat differently the role money plays in it. One might say that in Marx's imagery alienation arises from the relationship between three entities, none of which he thinks of primarily as "made of money": the factory as the visible embodiment of capital; labor power, vested in the worker but necessarily sold for a wage; and the commodity produced by means of wage labor. In this imagery money figures as the indispensable link connecting those entities: nothing less, but also nothing more. To Simmel, money is much more the protagonist of economic alienation; he recognizes, as we have seen (in chapter 5) the historical significance of the point at which money begins to function as capital, yet does not make money's essential properties (and its "alienative" potential) depend on that function.

Besides, Marx not only emphasizes economic alienation, but also tends to derive from it other forms of alienation (political and religious) or at least treats these, at any rate within modern society, as secondary and subsidiary to economic alienation. Simmel seems to disagree. While, as I repeat, he resolutely places money, and thus economic alienation, at the center of his picture of modern society, he emphatically denies

that, as "historical materialism" claims, economic phenomena have a general causal priority over others of a
nonmaterial nature (13; 56); and he holds to this theoretical position even as far as modern society is concerned. He explicitly refers to "the modern constitutional state" [*Rechtsstaat*], not to money, in a passage of
PdG which offers, to my mind, one of the sharpest con-
ceptualizations of the nature of alienation in general:
"The fact that it [the state] constitutes a synthesis of
differentiated components of individual subjects, visibly turns it into both an interpersonal and a superper-
sonal entity" (647; this passage is omitted in the English translation).

I come to a final, fundamental difference between
Marx's and Simmel's views on alienation. The two
thinkers, it seems to me, address the problem of alienation from very different value standpoints and with
very different moral preoccupations. Marx's moral vision is that of a revolutionary thinker who seeks to
guide the masses toward the fulfillment of a tremen-
dous task, "the solution of the riddle of history," the
construction of a totally new society, free of alienation,
on the ruins of the existent one; his sensitivity responds
chiefly to the collective suffering that motivates and justifies the revolutionary struggle of the working class.
What chiefly inspires Simmel, instead, is a lofty concern with individualistic values, and particularly with
the values implicit in the idea of "cultivation" as discussed above—values such as scholarly or scientific attainment, intellectual integrity, and aesthetic sensitivity. What he sees at stake in modern life, in particular, is
chiefly the individuals' capacity to reflect on, understand, appreciate, and evaluate the events that impinge

upon their direct experience, through participation in ordinary life or (preferably) through cultured and creative pursuits.

From this standpoint, one feels, Simmel largely ignores Marx's burning concerns. He seems to feel that the great machine of industrial capitalism can offer the masses enough opportunities to satisfy their more compelling needs, beyond which they are not likely to look, except to ask for more. He is no revolutionary, for he feels that the human critical plight is inscribed in the nature of man, which can find varying expression in history but cannot be radically changed. (Simmel is preeminently a dialectical thinker. But it has been said of his that it is "a dialectic without final reconciliation.") In any case, his concern is with the *quality* of life; and this is intrinsically, for him, an aspect of individual lived experience.

The prevalence of this concern in Simmel's thinking, and the fact that it is generally focused not on individuals at large, but on those relatively few individuals who have any chance at all to entertain what he considers a proper relationship with the world of objects, occasionally imparts a slightly disdainful, aristocratic tone to his argument. But one can forgive Simmel for that on a number of counts. First, the aristocracy he envisages (and feels himself a part of) is one of the intellect and the spirit, not one of blood. Second, typically that aristocracy fulfills its mission (if at all) by absorbing, interpreting, and adding to the universal human values embodied in "high culture," which often reflect upon the *lachrymae rerum*, the finitude and sadness of the human condition, so that *qui auget scientiam auget dolorem*, he who adds to his knowledge adds to his

suffering. Finally, there is, so to speak, a tragic undertone to that aristocratic overtone.

Although few enough are called to attempt that mission, fewer yet are elected to accomplish it; and even
their accomplishment can never be a permanent one.
Those very few must ever anew (I am translating the
emphatic, pathos-laden "immer wieder" of Simmel's
contemporary and kindred spirit, Rainer Maria Rilke)
defeat the temptations of superficiality, of narrow spe-
cialization, of sheer, all-too-human complacency and
pride over what they already know and what they have
already experienced and done.

To bring to a close this argument, and the book, I will
mention a few criticisms of the modern "quality of life"
voiced by Simmel in *PdG* from the value standpoint I
have indicated. First, the universal hold of the money
economy has a strong *devaluing* effect on the things that
money commands; to quote Oscar Wilde's famous aphorism, people know "the price of everything and the
value of nothing." Simmel phrases this criticism as follows: "The fact that ever more things can be had for
money, and the related one, that money becomes the
central and absolute value, has the consequence that
things eventually are only valued to the extent that they
cost money, and that the quality of value we see in them
is merely a function of their higher or lower money
price. . . . The significance of money replaces the significance of things" (369–70; *279*). A psychological correlate of this development is the growing prevalence, particularly within the upper strata of modern, urban
society, of what Simmel calls *Blasiertheit*—the blasé
attitude. This consists in the loss of a capacity for discriminating appreciation of values. The blasé person

"experiences all things as being equally dull and gray, as having nothing worth getting excited about" (334–35, *256*).

Second, the properties of money act back on the individuals who are, as it were, the titular protagonists of the economy and the society which find in money their center. Consider for instance the "characterlessness" of money. As David Frisby points out, there are frequent intimations in *PdG* of the emergence of a human type both celebrated and criticized in a famous Austrian novel, Robert Musil's *Man without Qualities.* Frisby writes: "Money's indifference to human goals and its facilitation of the reduction of individuals to fragmented functions . . . suggest that the individual has not merely lost control over one of the purest of social forms but is actually faced with his or her disintegration as a total personality. . . . Individuals . . . are unable to act except in order to perform . . . fragmented functions."[16]

Furthermore the centrality of the money economy, and, in association with this, the existence of multiple, lengthy means/goals chains, imparts to modern society a quality of growing abstractness and artificiality. Individuals deal with less and less concrete, down-to-earth experiences, as a result of the following progression. As we saw in chapter 3, economic value itself is based on a comparison established (with a view to exchange) between preexistent, primary values. But then money stands for economic value itself, and in this capacity becomes the medium of increasingly extensive and complex sets of transactions; furthermore, over time, money undergoes a process of increasing symbolization (see chapter 5, section IV). "As a result, what people under modern conditions tend to treat as "absolute value"—money itself—bears a more and more remote and abstract relation to economic, let alone, primary values: "the economic relations, priorities and fluctuations of concrete things appear as derivatives from their own derivative, that is as representatives and shadows of the significance which their money equivalent possesses" (181; *157*).

A significant implication of this is the growing economic significance of purely speculative activities in the financial market; these deprive of all stability the relation between the ultimate value of objects and its representation by, say, a bond or debenture bought or sold on the market for negotiable instruments. According to Simmel, such circumstances allow unrestricted play to "the psychological impulses of caprice, of greed, of ungrounded opinion" (438; *326*)—a view which cannot fail to strike a chord in those aware of the increasing significance of purely financial maneuverings in today's economy.

In sum, it is not just that, in modern society, "Things are in the saddle / And ride mankind" (a particularly effective statement of the phenomenon of inversion/alienation). The point is also that more and more of the "things" in question bear only an exceedingly remote and arbitrary relation to human feelings and wants. What seemed to Thoreau his contemporaries' foolish concern with dispensable possessions (see the opening section of *Walden*) is many times surpassed, on the evidence of *PdG*, by Simmel's contemporaries (and many times more by ours). According to Simmel, this imparts to the modern experience an increasing sense of unreality, of illusoriness, which he attributes also to the growing significance of technology (670; *481*). In a later essay he quoted Saint Francis's definition of the ideal attitude toward material things—*nihil habentes, omnia possidentes*—and suggested that the opposite applies to modern individuals: *omnia habentes, nihil possidentes*. Because modern technology is certainly superior to premodern, we are led to think of it as intrinsically significant; that is, we fail to ask ourselves what valuable ends it might assist us in achieving. Once more, this failure impoverishes the quality of our lived experience by centering it on matters and processes which should by rights lie at its periphery (672; *482*).

V

There are perhaps enough critical arguments in Simmel's discussion about modern society reviewed in this chapter, and they bear enough resemblance to typical arguments from what has been labeled the German "cultural pessimism,"[17] to make some readers think that Simmel shared the rejection of modernity characteristic of so many German intellectuals of his generation (as well as the previous one and a couple of later ones). In my opinion, this is not a tenable view. As I have tried to show, *Philosophie des Geldes* advances in fact a highly complex, differentiated view of modernity, whose negative components offset to an extent, but definitely do not overwhelm the positive ones. In particular, there is, I have argued, a "cognitive gain" in the modern perception of the intrinsically processual nature of reality and of the necessarily relativistic nature of knowledge. There is also what could be called an "institutional gain": particularly the position found in modern culture for the value of freedom and the extent to which the modern social structure, through the multiplicity of partly contrasting affiliations, fosters the growth of individuality. (This second argument is much better articulated in "The Web of Group Affiliations" than in *PdG*, which instead clearly and emphatically expounds the first).[18]

Simmel is nothing if not a complex author, with a particularly keen eye for nuances and for implausible equilibria between apparently contradictory motifs. For instance, some of the very passages that emphasize the numerous, insidious traps modernity lays on the path of individuals toward true cultivation also suggest that often only the possession of money, as a particularly abstract, symbolic, objective, impersonal resource, allows those individuals even to start down that path; for money disengages them from economic interests that would too closely affect their personalities and narrow their horizons. Thus, modernity, for Simmel, bears both a threat and a promise. The "tragedy of culture," as I have already suggested, lies in the fact that there is, so to speak, an asymmetry of probability as concerns the realization respectively of the threat or the promise. But those very few individuals who can—*immer wieder*—fulfil the promise represent, in Simmel's aristocratic judgment, a precious and sophisticated embodiment of universal human potentialities.

Notes

Chapter 1

1. See Reinhard Bendix, *Kings or People: Power and the Mandate to Rule*, University of California Press, Berkeley, 1978.

2. See Francis L. Carsten, *Princes and Parliaments in Germany from the Fifteenth to the Eighteenth Century*, Clarendon Press, Oxford, 1959.

3. For the origins of these arrangements, see Hans Rosenberg, *Bureaucracy, Aristocracy, and Autocracy: The Prussian Experience, 1669–1815*, Harvard University Press, Cambridge, 1958.

4. See Alexander Gerschenkron, *Bread and Democracy in Germany*, University of California Press, Berkeley, 1943.

5. See the discussion of Germany in Barrington Moore, Jr., *Injustice: The Social Bases of Obedience and Revolt*, Macmillan, London, 1978.

6. Klaus Epstein, *Matthias Erzeberger and the Dilemma of German Democracy*, Princeton University Press, Princeton, 1959, 20.

7. For a thoroughgoing critique of the line of argument I have pursued so far and am now seeking to qualify somewhat, see David Blackbourn and Geoffrey Eley, *Peculiarities of German History: Bourgeois Society and Politics in Nineteenth Century Germany*, Oxford University Press, New York, 1984.

8. Hajo Holborn, "Der deutsche Idealismus in sozialgeschichtlicher Beleuchtung," *Historische Zeitschrift* 174 (1952): 378.

9. See Moore, *Injustice*, 387.

10. See H. S. Hughes, *Consciousness and Society: The Reorientation of European Social Thought, 1890–1920*, Knopf, New York, 1956.

11. See Theodore M. Porter, *The Rise of Statistical Thinking: 1820–1990*, Princeton University Press, Princeton, 1986, esp. ch. 6.

12. Hans Freyer, *Theorie des objektiven Geistes: eine Einleitung in die Kulturphilosophie*, Teubner, Leipzig, 1923, 2–3.

13. Pietro Rossi, *Lo storicismo tedesco contemporaneo*, Einaudi, Turin, 1957.

14. See R. Koselleck, "Fortschritt," in *Geschichtliche Grundbegriffe: Historisches Lexikon zur politischen-sozialen Sprache in Deutschland*, Klett, Stuttgart, 1972–, vol. 2.

15. Quoted in Gerhard Masur, *Imperial Berlin*, Basic Books, New York, 1978, 196.

16. Wolfgang Lepenies, *Die drei Kulturen: Soziologie zwischen Literatur und Wissenschaft*, Hanser, Munich, 1985, 245.

17. Quoted in Wilhelm Hennis, *Max Webers Fragestellung: Studien zur Biographie des Werkes*, Mohr, Tübingen, 1987, 142.

18. *Exerzierfeld der Moderne: Industriekultur im 19. Jahrhundert*, ed. Jochen Boberg et al., Beck, Munich, 1984, 144.

19. Masur, *Imperial Berlin*, 176.

20. Pierangelo Schiera, *Il laboratorio borghese: scienza e politica nella Germania dell' Ottocento*, Mulino, Bologna, 1987, 322.

21. Quoted in David Frisby, *Sociological Impressionism: A Reassessment of Georg Simmel's Social Theory*, Heinemann, London, 1981, 25.

22. Masur, *Imperial Berlin*, 201.

Chapter 2

1. Monika Richarz, "Judisches Berlin und seine Vernichtung," in *Die Metropole: Industriekultur in Berlin im 20. Jahrhundert*, ed. Jochen Boberg et al., Beck, Munich, 1986, 216 (my translation).

2. Masur, *Imperial Berlin*, 110.

3. Ibid., 118.

4. René König, "Die Juden und die Soziologie," in *Soziologie in Deutschland: Begründer, Verfechter, Verächter,* Hanser, Munich, 1987, 330.

5. Other cases are occasionally discussed, as, for instance, in the Max Weber correspondence of 1906 to 1908, now available in Max Weber, *Briefe 1906–1908,* Mohr (Siebeck), Tübingen, 1990.

6. See Wolfgang Dressen, "Berliner Freiheit," in Boberg, *Exerzierfeld der Modern,* 30–38.

7. See Lewis Coser, "The Stranger in the Academy," in *Georg Simmel,* ed. Lewis Coser, Prentice-Hall, Englewood Cliffs, N.J., 1965.

8. Frisby, *Sociological Impressionism,* 13.

9. See Johannes Weiss, "Georg Simmel, Max Weber, und die 'Soziologie,'" in *Simmel und die frühen Soziologen: Nähe und Distanz zu Durkheim, Tönnies und Max Weber,* ed. Otthein Ramstedt, Suhrkamp, Frankfurt, 1988, 36–63.

10. Cited in Frisby, *Sociological Impressionism,* 33.

11. For an exception, see a letter from Simmel to the French sociologist Celestin Bouglé, reprinted in Lepenies, *Die drei Kulturen,* 225.

12. See Hans-Joachim Lieber, *Kulturkritik und Lebensphilosophie: Studien zur deutschen Philosophie der Jahrhundertwende,* Wissenschaftliche Buchgesellschaft, Darmstadt, 1974, 67–105.

13. Paul Schnabel, "Georg Simmel," in Dirk Käsler, ed., *Klassikers des soziologischen Denkens,* vol. 1, Beck, Munich, 1976, 262.

14. On the question of the mutual bearing of economics and *The Philosophy of Money,* see David Frisby, "Some Economic Aspects of *The Philosophy of Money,*" ch. 5 of *Simmel and Since: Essays on Georg Simmel's Social Theory,* Routledge, London, 1991.

15. See Joseph Schumpeter, *History of Economic Analysis,* Oxford University Press, New York, 1954, 814.

16. "Preface to the Second Edition," in Georg Simmel, *The Philosophy of Money,* ed. David Frisby, Routledge, London, 1990, xxi.

17. Ibid.

18. Max Weber, "Simmel as Sociologist," *Social Research* 39 (1972): 159. On the relationship between the two, see David Frisby, "The Ambiguity of Modernity: Georg Simmel and Max Weber," in *Max Weber and His Contemporaries*, ed. Wolfgang J. Mommsen and Jurgen Ostehammel, Unwin Hyman, London, 1987, 422–33. See also S. Segre, *Weber contro Simmel: L'epistemologia di Simmel alla prova della sociologia comprendente*, ECIG, Milano, 1987.

19. The review is available in English as "Georg Simmel, Philosophie des Geldes," in *Emile Durkheim: Contributions to L'Année Sociologique*, ed. Yash Nandan, Free Press, New York, 1980, 94–98.

20. Frisby, "Preface to the Second Edition," in Simmel, *The Philosophy of Money*, xxiii.

21. Quoted in Frisby, *Sociological Impressionism*, 24.

Chapter 3

1. Talcott Parsons, *The Structure of Social Action: A Study in Social Theory with Special Reference to a Group of Recent European Writers*, McGraw-Hill, New York, 1937.

2. Frisby, *Sociological Impressionism*, 3–4.

3. See, for example, the section on "alienated labor" in Karl Marx, *Texte zu Methode und Praxis: Pariser Manuskripte*, Rowohlt, Reinbek, 1868, 50–62.

4. George Sorel, "Letter to Daniel Halévy," in *Reflections on Violence* (1906), Peter Smith, New York, 1941, 30–31.

5. Alessandro Cavalli and Lucio Perucchi, "Introduzione," in Georg Simmel, *Filosofia del denaro*, UTET, 1984, 17.

6. Parsons, *Structure of Social Action*, e.g., 141, 253.

7. Norbert Elias, *The Civilizing Process: Sociogenetic and Psychogenetic Investigations*, Blackwell, Oxford, 1982.

8. The problem of the knowledge of other selves is raised in Georg Simmel, *Die Probleme der Geschichtsphilosophie: Eine erkenntnistheoretische Studie*, 5th ed., Duncker & Humblot, Munich, 1923, 88, 109.

9. Parsons, *Structure of Social Action*, 258ff.

10. On the relationship between *value* and *values* see Martin Albrow, *Max Weber's Construction of Social Theory*, St. Martin's Press, New York, 1990, 227–29.

11. Max Weber, *Economy and Society*, Bedminster Press, Totowa, N.J., 1967, 64.

Chapter 4

1. Frisby, *Sociological Impressionism*, 15.

2. Michael Landmann, "Georg Simmel: Konturen seines Denkens," in *Aesthetik und Soziologie um die Jahrhundertwende: Georg Simmel*, cited in Cavalli and Perucchi, "Introduzione," in Simmel, *Filosofia del denaro*, 32n.42.

3. *Dictionary of Philosophy*, ed. Antony Flew, Macmillan, London, 1979, s.v. "Spirit."

4. On the "hermeneutical circle," see Simmel, *Probleme der Geschichtsphilosophie*, 26–28.

5. Karel Kosik, *Dialectics of the Concrete: A Study of the Problem of Man and the World*, Reidel, Dordrecht, 1967, ch. 5.

6. The most relevant works of Arnold Gehlen in this context are probably *Man, His Nature and His Place in the World*, Columbia University Press, New York, 1984; and *Urmensch und Spätkultur*, Athenaeum, Frankfurt, 1964. For a very succinct secondary presentation, see Peter Berger, "Foreword," in Gehlen, *Man in the Age of Technology*, Columbia University Press, New York, 1980.

7. See Jerry Z. Muller, *The Other God that Failed: Hans Freyer and the Deradicalization of German Conservatism*, Princeton University Press, Princeton, 1987. See also Jeffrey Herf, *Reactionary Modernism: Technology, Culture and Politics in Weimar and the Third Reich*, Columbia University Press, New York, 1984.

8. Hannah Arendt, *The Human Condition*, Doubleday, Garden City, N.Y., 1959, 82–83.

9. See Karl Popper, *The Open Society and Its Enemies*, Routledge, London, 1945.

10. Now in Karl Popper, *Objective Knowledge: An Evolutionary Approach*, Oxford University Press, Oxford, 1972; page references in the text are to this edition.

11. The similarity appears even greater if one considers a passage of Simmel's *Probleme der Geschichtsphilosophie*, 133.

12. Quoted in Simmel, *Probleme der Geschichtsphilosophie*, 46.

Chapter 5

1. Janet L. Abu-Lughod, *Before European Hegemony*, Oxford University Press, New York, 1989, ch. 7.

2. Karl Polanyi, *The Great Transformation*, Beacon, Boston, 1957.

Chapter 6

1. For a thoroughgoing exploration of the roots of this problem in the history of Western ideas, see Hans Blumenberg, *The Legitimacy of the Modern Age*, MIT Press, Cambridge, 1983.

2. Cavalli and Perucchi, "Introduzione," in Simmel *Filosofia del denaro*, 23.

3. David Frisby and Derek Sayer, *Society*, Norwood-Ellis, Chichester, 1986, 64.

4. Ibid., 55.

5. Ibid., 61.

6. See *Georg Simmel on Individuality and Social Forms*, ed. Donald Levine, University of Chicago Press, Chicago, 1971, ch. 9.

7. For a relatively diffuse statement of a distinctively modern conception of knowledge which emphasizes its superiority over premodern ones, see Simmel, *Probleme der Geschichtsphilosophie*, 53–58.

8. Raymond Boudon, "La teoria della conoscenza nella *Filosofia del denaro* di Simmel," *Rassegna italiana di sociologia* 30, 4 (October 1989): 47ff.

9. Ibid., 53.

10. A preference for "as if" statements is restated in Simmel, *Probleme der Geschichtsphilosophie*, 213.

11. "Introduction" to Levine, *Simmel on Individuality*, xxxv.

12. See Martin Bernal, *Black Athena: African and Asian Roots of Classical Civilization*, Free Press, London, 1987.

Chapter 7

1. See Georg Simmel, "Der Begriff und die Tragödie der Kultur," in *Das individuelle Gesetz: Philosophische Exkurse*, Suhrkamp, Frankfurt, 1968, 116–147.

2. On these concepts, see John Torrance, *Estrangement, Alienation and Exploitation: A Sociological Approach to Historical Materialism*, Macmillan, London, 1977.

3. See Arnold Gehlen, "Über dem Geburt der Freiheit aus der Entfremdung," in *Studien zu Anthropologie und Soziologie*, 2d ed., Luchterhand, Neuwied, 1971, 256ff.

4. Pierre Naville, *De l'aliénation à la jouissance: La genèse de la sociologie du travail chez Marx et Engels*, Anthropos, Paris, 1967.

5. Andrew Gamble and Paul Walton, *From Alienation to Surplus Value*, Sheed & Ward, London, 1972.

6. Yves Calvez, *La pensée de Karl Marx*, Seuil, Paris, 1956.

7. Karl Marx, *L'ideologia tedesca*, Editori Riuniti, Rome, 1975, 69–70.

8. Karl Marx, *Das Kapital*, vol. 1, ed. H.-J. Lieber and B. Kautsky, Cotta, Stuttgart, 1962, 30–31.

9. See Robert Michels, *Political Parties: A Sociological Study of the Oligarchical Tendencies of Modern Democracies*, Free Press, Glencoe, Ill., 1949.

10. See Peter Berger and Thomas Luckmann, *The Social Construction of Reality*, Doubleday, Garden City, N.Y., 1966, 78ff.

11. Simmel, "Begriff und Tragödie," 135.

12. Ibid., 143.

13. Karl Marx, "Die entfremdete Arbeit," in *Texte zu Methode und Praxis*, 50–62.

14. On the question of how much Simmel knew about Marx, see Kurt Lenk, "Soziologie und Ideologienlehre: Bemerkungen zur Marxismusdiskussion in der deutschen Soziologie von Simmel bis Mannheim," *Kölner Zeitschrift für Soziologie und Sozialpsychologie* 13 (1961): 261ff.

15. See "Der Konflikt der modernen Kultur," in Simmel, *Individuelle Gesetz*, 148–177.

16. Frisby, *Sociological Impressionism*, 146.

17. See Stephen Kalberg, "The Origin and Expansion of *Kulturpessimismus:* The Relationship between Public and Private Spheres in Early Twentieth Century Germany," *Sociological Theory* 5 (Fall 1987): 150ff.

18. See the chapter from *Soziologie* translated by Reinhard Bendix as "The Web of Group Affiliations" in Georg Simmel, *Conflict and the Web of Group Affliations*, Free Press, Glencoe, Ill., 1956.

Index

Philosophy of Money (Simmel): alienation in, 185, 197; author's promotional essay on, 62–68; genesis of, 56–60; importance in modern sociology, 164; on modernism, 165, 167–69, 171–74, 211–12; organization of text, 60–62; publication of (1900), 40, 47, 59; revised edition (1907), 60; translation of, 1, 56, 61, 69
Planck, Max, 35
Plato, 90, 128, 130; *Crito*, 192
Polanyi, Karl, 163
Political Parties (Michels), 190
Political system, German: unmodernized, 18–19, 37, 164
Popper, Karl: Hegel, 125, 128; "Epistemology without a Knowing Subject," 126; and objective spirit, 125–28; "On the Theory of the Objective Mind," 126; *The Open Society and Its Enemies*, 128; on human action, 129
Precious metals: as money, 159–60
"Problem of Sociology, The" (Simmel), 47
Prussia: archaic social and political system, 5–6, 10; dominance in the German empire, 2–3, 7; unifies Germany, 6–7, 9
"Psychology of Money, The" (Simmel), 57

Ranke, Otto von, 16
Relativism: and "German ideology," 53; of knowledge, 170–72; Simmel on, 171–72
Religion: and money, 176, 182
Research, scientific and technical, 14–15
Rickert, Heinrich, 57, 69

Rilke, Rainer Maria, 208
Robbery, 98–99
Rousseau, Jean-Jacques, 186, 187
Royal Opera (Berlin), 35

Schmoller, Gustav, 31–32, 56–58
Shakespeare, William: *Othello*, 145–47
Simmel, Georg: academic career, 39–40, 43–44, 52, 56; on aesthetics, 94; on alienation, 185, 188–91, 193–94, 200–201, 203–7; and antisemitism, 40–41, 43–44; *Basic Questions of Sociology: Individual and Society*, 47; as a Berliner, 32, 37, 38; concept of society, 166–67; concept of sociology, 48–51; "The Concept and Tragedy of Culture," 185, 194, 196, 199, 202; correlates money with liberal democracy, 152–53; on democratic character of money, 151–52; on economic action, 95–103, 132; on exchange, 134–35; family background, 38–39; and *Historismus*, 52; on human action, 71–72, 75–77, 85; on individuality, 166; on judgments of fact and value, 86–88, 99–100; on labor, 101; on Marx, 202–3; "The Metropolis and Mental Life," 38, 197; on modernism, 52–54, 165, 167–68, 169, 171, 174–75, 176; on money, 134–35, 137, 139–45, 147, 149–52, 155–58, 161, 178, 181–82; and nature of knowledge, 168, 170–71, 174; Nazis destroy his papers, 54; on objective spirit, 108–12, 112–13, 117,

Compositor: BookMasters, Inc.
Text: 11/15 Aster
Display: Gill Sans
Printer and Binder: BookCrafters, Inc.